# FUNERALS to Die For

# FUNERALS to Die For

## THE CRAZIEST, CREEPIEST, AND MOST BIZARRE FUNERAL TRADITIONS AND PRACTICES EVER

KATHY BENJAMIN

Published by
Adams Media, a division of F+W Media, Inc.
57 Littlefield Street, Avon, MA 02322. U.S.A.
*www.adamsmedia.com*

ISBN 10: 1-4405-5707-1
ISBN 13: 978-1-4405-5707-1
eISBN 10: 1-4405-5708-X
eISBN 13: 978-1-4405-5708-8

Printed in the United States of America.

10 9 8 7 6 5 4 3 2 1



*This book is available at quantity discounts for bulk purchases.*
*For information, please call 1-800-289-0963.*

# DEDICATION

To Simon

# ACKNOWLEDGMENTS

This book would not have been possible without the help of so many amazing people. I would like to thank my husband Simon for managing to wrap his scientific brain around the craziness writers exist in and for all the time he spent helping make this book the best it could be. Halli, my lovely editor, without whom this book never would have existed, for her patience and endlessly positive e-mails, as well as holding my hand through this whole crazy process. I'd like to thank all the family and friends who kept me sane and contributed ideas, whether online or in person. I'd like to thank my Mom and Dad for putting up with me for thirty years, and my sister Lisa for not asking me to edit her master's thesis the week this book's first draft was due.

Thank you to all the editors who got me to this point in my career, particularly those at Cracked.com and Mental Floss. Without you guys I would still be working retail. I owe each of you my firstborn, so here's hoping I have septuplets.

Finally to everyone who has read my work and everyone who bought this book, thank you so, so much.

TABLE OF
CONTENTS

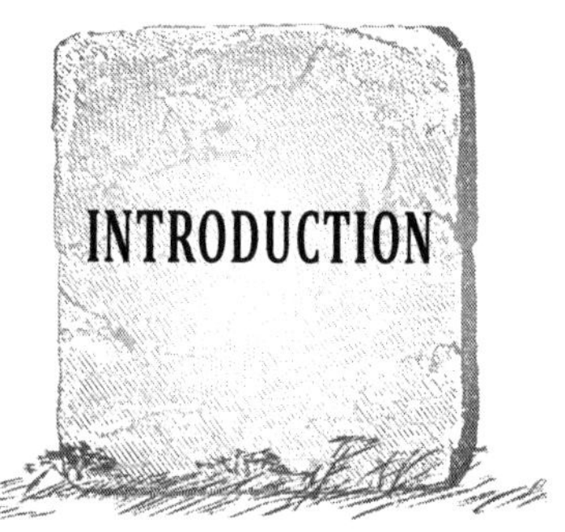


You are going to die.

It's true and it's something that everyone has to come to terms with eventually. You will die, and no matter what afterlife or lack thereof you think you are headed for, the body you left behind suddenly needs to be disposed of as quickly as possible.

If you managed to come to terms with your mortality at some point, you might have left behind a will outlining what you would like to happen to your corpse. And if you are like the large majority of people in the world, you will have selected something really boring, like a standard church burial or cremation with your ashes being spread somewhere pretty. But what you might not know is that there are dozens of other options out there; everything from the environmentally friendly to the creepy to the downright illegal. Why not start some crazy new traditions or borrow some of the crazier ones from other cultures? You want some leather pants made out of a friend? No problem. "I'm Too Sexy" by Right Said Fred might not seem like your typical mourning song, but it is a lot more popular than you'd think, so go ahead and request that a DJ spin it as your coffin is lowered into the grave. You always wanted to go into space? Don't let the tiny inconvenience of being dead stop you. After all, there are 7 billion people on the planet right now and every single one of them will need a funeral one day. Let's make them awesome!

*Funerals to Die For* takes a look at more than 100 of the weird, creepy, and slightly gross ways that people have dealt with death for thousands of years. So settle in—maybe not right before or after a meal just to be safe—and let's put the fun back in funeral! Enjoy!

# THE HILARIOUS HISTORY OF INHUMATION

While you would think burying your dead would be pretty self-explanatory (dig a hole and then cry over it for a bit), history proves that there is no limit to the human imagination, especially when it comes to getting rid of dead bodies. Ever since humanity came up with the idea of mourning their dead they have been trying to perfect the process, and stumbling on some pretty bizarre rituals along the way. While some of the things that started out as crazy and slightly gross ways of dealing with corpses have now become commonplace, like cremation, other fads, like taking formal portraits of dead people, are hopefully best left to history. And while eating your relatives out of love may seem weird, do you really think what goes into embalming a corpse is any less gross? (The answer is no, not really.)

# THE FIRST BURIALS

Ritual burial practices tell archaeologists a lot about humanity. In fact, burying people in symbolic ways, as opposed to just dumping the body because it smells bad, is considered by most paleoanthropologists to be directly tied to many other important developments in human behavior. As *Homo sapiens* began to develop language and religious beliefs they also started coming up with ideas about death and the afterlife, at which point we get well thought-out graves.

Humans are not the only animals to have some sort of burial practice, but we are by far the most complex about it. While elephants may return to their elephant graveyards to die, it can be argued that humans started becoming human the first time they added items to a grave for no other reason than so the corpse, or at least their spirit, would still have access to those things. While there is evidence that some prehuman prodigies may have started adding a flint knife or two to graves as many as 320,000 years ago, it was only about 100,000 years ago that ritual burial really took off. Once humans developed language they could explain their ideas about life and death to others, and one tribe could then explain those beliefs to other people as well. Soon humans were all digging graves and adding burial items in the hopes that the spirit of the dead would be happy in the afterlife. Suddenly people had a connection to their dead; they were no longer just bodies, but something to be respected with funeral rites.

Still it took a long time until every culture had a set religion and the burial rituals to go with them. By about 12,000 years ago every culture had their own special way of disposing of their dead, but these techniques changed drastically over the next twelve millennia and continue to change significantly today. Emerging technologies allow us to dispose of bodies in ways our ancestors could not possibly have dreamed of. In fact, it was only about 100 years ago that cremation became acceptable in the Western world, and today, the funeral business is a billion-dollar-a-year industry. While people may have huge differences in what we do and don't believe, one thing unites us all as humans: When those corpses show up we are going to dispose of them based on 100,000 years of increasingly complex rituals. Simple right? Read and be amazed my friends, read on.

**HE IS ONE OF THOSE PEOPLE WHO WOULD BE ENORMOUSLY IMPROVED BY DEATH.**

H. H. MUNRO (SAKI), AUTHOR (DIED 1916)

# NOT-SO-FINAL RESTING PLACES

For as long as people have been burying their dead, there have been other people coming along and digging them right back up. While some stole the bodies themselves, most were after the sweet loot buried with the deceased. Almost every Egyptian king's pyramid or tomb was robbed numerous times within decades of their death in order to get at all the treasure held within. The graves of Chinese aristocrats were robbed so often that for centuries archaeologists thought the jade burial suits ancient chroniclers went on about were just a legend.

One of the strangest grave robbing sprees occurred over a three-year period during the 1860s in Salt Lake City, Utah. While you can probably at least understand why people in need of some extra dough or some slightly weird professional criminals would dig up graves in order to find valuables to resell, Jean Baptiste—a local gravedigger—did it for the love of fashion. And also because he was pretty bonkers.

Baptiste's crimes might never have been discovered, but in 1862 a police officer shot and killed three criminals. The families of two of the men took care of their relatives' burials, but the third body went unclaimed. A charitable local offered to pay for appropriate burial attire for the man and the criminal was interred in the Salt Lake City cemetery. A few months later his brother heard what happened and asked the body be dug up and moved to a different cemetery. Everyone involved was shocked when they opened the coffin and the corpse was completely naked. Not even a bowtie or a sombrero.

Having no idea where to start looking for the culprit, the cemetery's owner recommended the police ask John Baptiste if he had seen anyone weird hanging around. When the cops showed up at John's house he wasn't home, but his wife let them in. Described later as a "simple-minded woman" it obviously didn't seem weird to her that there were boxes all over the house filled with "flesh soiled" clothes, but the police noticed immediately. The well-attired Baptiste was arrested and accused of robbing more than 300 corpses of their dignity.

Brigham Young, then the head of the Mormon Church and Governor of the Utah Territory, didn't want to make a big deal out of the embarrassing crime, so he reassured his followers that if they reburied all the clothes in one large grave, then all of their relatives would be raised up at the end times fully clothed—not with their junk hanging out for Jesus to point and laugh at. This saved him from having to dig up the entire cemetery looking for naked corpses, although asking for volunteers to help probably would have weeded out some sickos pretty quickly. Young also made sure the local newspapers downplayed the incident, and convinced everyone that Baptiste should be banished, not executed. As punishment, history's most fashionable grave robber was sent to an inhospitable island in the middle of a lake, but not before he got some pretty unfashionable new ink. As part of his punishment, the words "Branded for Robbing the Dead" were tattooed across his forehead. It would have taken some really Lady Gaga–esque outfits to distract people from that face tattoo—or at least a crowd of inmates from a maximum security jail.

# CITY OF THE DEAD

If you ever find yourself in one of the more war-torn parts of Russia, there is a chance that you will end up on a three-hour bus ride, then hiking for miles, and finally arriving in a town of tiny houses full of dead people. Needless to say, Russian vodka is a hell of a beverage, and the more you drink, the more likely the chance of this field trip becomes.

The "town" of Dargavs is really a necropolis (literally "city of the dead") in North Ossetia, and its couple dozen houses that look like they came out of a fairy tale were only ever used to house the dead, or at least people who were going to be heading that way very soon. Adding to the surreal creepiness of this isolated area is the surrounding mountain terrain that is virtually desolate and gives the area a very claustrophobic atmosphere. To make things even weirder, many of the dead are laid out in wooden boats, an odd touch, since there are no navigable rivers in the area. Apparently the locals believed the dead had to cross a river to get to the afterlife, so they helped them out.

***The "town" of Dargavs is really a necropolis (literally "city of the dead") in North Ossetia, and its houses that look like they came out of a fairy tale were only ever used to house the dead, or at least people who were going to be heading that way very soon.***

The ninety-five "houses" with their white brick walls and peaked roofs look like they should be home to Snow White's dwarves. The only slightly eerie thing about them is the fact that they all have only one tiny window. If your hindbrain isn't screaming at you by now to leave and find the nearest bar, you might be tempted to look inside. You'll see almost nothing, except a couple of skeletons and the last shred of your sanity.

Starting in the 1600s, plague ravaged the area. By the 1800s, the population of the local area was down to 16,000 from a high of 200,000. While the mountain ridge had been a local cemetery since the 1400s, once the plague hit, building the structures there became a necessity. In some cases people who had lost all their family to the disease and had no one left to bury them when they died would enter one of the houses and wait for the inevitable. Others went as soon as they knew they were ill in order to isolate themselves from the rest of the population. Kind locals would push bread through the tiny windows and if the sick survived the plague they would return home. As the buildings became a more common sight on the mountain, families would build their own house-tomb for relatives who had already passed away.

Walking through a literal ghost town covered in fog is a pretty creepy experience, and local lore says that anyone who goes to the city will not come out alive. Presumably this does not include the people who go there to inter their loved ones, or one funeral could wipe out an entire family—if the plague didn't get to them first.

**I'M TRYING TO DIE CORRECTLY, BUT IT'S VERY DIFFICULT, YOU KNOW.**

LAWRENCE DURRELL, AUTHOR (DIED 1990)

# CATACOMBS

In the Middle Ages, Paris became a very popular place to live. Unfortunately for those people who liked to keep their days dead body free, French logic dictated it was therefore also a popular place to die. As urban sprawl built up right next to churches they lost the ability to expand their cemeteries, but people still wanted to be buried there, room be damned, because even after death no one wanted to have to leave the beautiful city for the suburbs. Soon even the city's largest cemetery was overcrowded with human remains. Water supplies were tainted, and the smell was unbearable. There was simply not enough room for the dead to keep on taking up space next to the living.

Fortunately, someone pointed out that Paris already had tunnels under much of the city, left over from mining attempts centuries before. From 1786 to 1788 the people of the City of Lights exhumed virtually all of their dead and stored them in the newly consecrated catacombs. Because Parisians abhor plain décor, soon the bones were being arranged to make walls 10 feet tall, lining much of the tunnels. There was plenty of building material, as the remains of an estimated 6 million people are stored down there. Almost immediately the catacombs became a popular tourist attraction, and at least one person is supposed to have gotten lost and died down there in 1793. During World War II both the French Resistance and the Nazis used the tunnels for war work (imagine the videogame *Doom* in real life). While still popular today, the tunnels did prevent almost any tall buildings from being built in Paris, since a large enough foundation would have destroyed parts of them.

***. . . soon the bones were being arranged to make walls 10 feet tall, lining much of the tunnels.***

While there is something about walls of anonymous bones that does make you feel completely insignificant, the Capuchin Catacombs of Palermo definitely one-up Paris on the creepiness factor. In the 1500s a monastery in the Italian city ran out of room in their own cemetery and dug out a crypt below it. Using some very original techniques, they dried out the bodies of dead monks naturally in the catacombs and put them on display in their best clothing. Soon wealthy people in the area decided this sounded a lot more fun than just being put in the ground to rot—after all, what good were expensive burial clothes if no one was able to see them? In exchange for donations the monks started letting other people be laid to rest under their monastery, even decking the bodies out in new fashions as the styles changed.

Families were invited to come visit their relatives as long as they kept up the payments. If the money stopped flowing in, the monks would move the body from its shelf and put it in a more out of the way place. Eventually there were so many dead that the monks organized them into different areas, with wings of the catacombs dedicated only to women, children, and virgins, among others. While interments stopped in the 1920s, you can still visit the dead. Most of them are laid out on shelves lining the walls, but some better-preserved ones are hung from hooks, and a few families even had their relative placed in a pose for all eternity.

# THE TERRACOTTA ARMY

In 221 B.C., Qin Shi Huang became the first emperor of a united China at the tender age of thirteen. While most prepubescent boys today would be thinking about the girl they have a crush on and how to convince their parents to buy them the latest video game system, Qin knew what was really important in life: death. Or more importantly, how he would be remembered after death. That's why almost immediately upon taking the throne he ordered that construction begin on his seriously gargantuan tomb, one that inspires awe to this day.

Eventually Qin would grow from a boy to a king worthy of such a grand tomb. He picked the spot for his burial because the land in the area was full of gold and jade mines, items he deemed worthy of his awesomeness. Despite having 700,000 men work on his tomb for the rest of his life, as Qin got older he started freaking out about the prospect of actually inhabiting it one day and tried to force the greatest minds in his kingdom to find the secret to the elixir of life. While it would have been impressive if they had actually succeeded, it would have been a shame for one of the greatest tombs in history to go to waste. And in fact, the tomb didn't stay empty for long; Qin was only forty-nine when he was entombed in his great mausoleum.

So just what sort of place was he going to spend the rest of eternity in? First of all, it was more than 12,000 square feet. Dozens of rooms were set aside to hold some of the greatest treasures the world had ever seen. A garden was constructed, with the leaves of trees made from solid jade. The dome of the tomb was studded with pearls inlaid in precious blue stones to look like stars in the night sky. A "river" was made of mercury, which means that if anyone in the tomb wasn't already dead, they would be almost immediately. But the most famous part of Qin's tomb was the 8,000 terracotta soldiers crafted to stand guard outside. Every single figure is unique, with its own hairstyle and facial expression. Each soldier has a rank, and some have horses.

While much of the tomb has been excavated since its rediscovery in the 1970s, archaeologists haven't even tried to get near the burial chamber, mostly because they assume whatever they find in there will be so valuable it will be almost impossible to guard. With riches like that it is no wonder Qin was so afraid to leave them behind. What's Chinese for "you can't take it with you"?

> **THEY SAY SUCH NICE THINGS ABOUT PEOPLE AT THEIR FUNERALS THAT IT MAKES ME SAD TO REALIZE THAT I'M GOING TO MISS MINE BY JUST A FEW DAYS.**
>
> GARRISON KEILLOR, AUTHOR AND RADIO PERSONALITY

# DRINKS ARE ON THE DEAD GUY

Funerals may be times for mourning, but the people hosting are still expected to feed those attending. Just because the guy in the coffin won't be eating anymore doesn't mean everyone else doesn't want some finger food and alcohol to take the edge off the whole event. This, combined with the fact that most people don't know every friend of their deceased relative on sight, means that complete strangers with absolutely no shame have managed to get a good meal off bereaved families for centuries.

These funeral crashers are called placebos. (And yes, our modern-day usage of *placebo* comes from these people, who would "deceive to please," just like fake pills do.) In the Catholic prayer cycle the Office of the Dead, the first thing the congregation sings is *placebo Domino in regione vivorum* ("I will please the Lord in the land of the living"). Eventually the people who attended and sang the rite became known as "placebo singers" after the first word of the prayer. Strangers doing this just to get the free meal were apparently commonplace by the 1300s, since Chaucer includes a reference to them in *The Canterbury Tales*, but the practice continues to this day. Since most funerals are ostensibly public events and are even announced in papers or church bulletins, nothing stops people from showing up. And even if the family is concerned about gatecrashers, they obviously have more on their minds at the time than making sure everyone who grabs a vol-au-vent actually spoke to the deceased at least once during his or her lifetime.

The Polish author Witold Gombrowicz lived in poverty in Argentina and is reported to have used funerals as free buffets during the 1950s and '60s. In 2007, the English television presenter Victoria Coren heard about a group attending funerals for the free booze and set out to catch them. She placed a fake obituary for the nonexistent Sir William Ormerod in the papers, making sure to point out it was "followed by a drinks reception." The freeloaders contacted her looking for tickets to attend the service, insisting they knew the figment of her imagination and he really would have wanted them to get plastered on his dime one last time.

The most notorious placebo in recent years was an artist named Reese Tong from New Zealand. Funeral directors there nicknamed him the "Grim Eater" due to his penchant for showing up at as many as four memorial services a week in order to score free food. Not content with just partaking while he was there, he also brought Tupperware containers in a backpack and when the hosts weren't looking packed up leftovers. It didn't take long for the people in charge to realize that this man couldn't possibly know all of these dead people. They pulled him aside and told him to stay away. When that didn't work they started warning others about him and eventually his photo and MO was sent to all funeral homes in the area. To be fair, he did at least put in some effort, always arriving nicely dressed and paying his respects with the rest of the mourners. At least he gets an A for effort.

# UNDEAD BURIAL PRECAUTIONS

In the Middle Ages, Europe had a problem. Sure sanitation was nonexistent, there was the whole Black Death thing, the mortality rate wasn't great, and medicine was rudimentary to say the least, but the real problem was the increasing number of vampires. People just would not stop rising from the dead. At least that's what a friend of a friend said, and if you can't trust the secondhand word of a person you've never met, who can you trust?

It was never the nice, hardworking people that seemed to reanimate either, so when undesirables (strangers, murderers, single women, etc.) died suddenly or mysteriously their bodies were often prepared in a way that kept them from coming back as vampires or zombies and killing people. Every area had its own original twist on the burial ritual, adding a bit of ethnic flair to vampire prevention. It's like local cuisine; what might seem like a perfectly lovely way of mutilating a dead body in France would go over about as well as frog legs in Russia.

Possibly the earliest attempts to keep the dead from rising up occurred in Ireland around A.D. 700, which is impressive, since it would be hundreds of years before anyone even coined the word "vampire" and hundreds more before Stephenie Meyer ruined them forever by making them sparkly. Archaeologists recently uncovered two skeletons buried separately, both of whom had large stones in their mouth. And these weren't stones that might have settled there over the last 1,300 years; this was a deliberate attempt to keep the dead in the ground. The stones were wedged in violently, with one almost dislocating the man's jaw. Still, it probably hurt less than a trip to the orthodontist. The large-stone-in-mouth technique must have worked to keep those guys in the ground, because it had some serious staying power. A different archaeological team found a skeleton from the 1500s with a brick shoved in its mouth in Italy, so undead technology obviously hadn't moved on much in 700 years or 1,000 miles.

Of course the most famous way of keeping a vampire down is a stake through the heart, and that did happen in real life, not just bad gothic novels. In 2012, two new corpses were added to the list of about a hundred already discovered in Bulgaria with wooden or metal rods driven through their bodies. Bulgarians were obviously desperately in need of some introductory courses on how to put rocks in mouths.

But before you laugh at those crazy medieval people and their tiny brains, the same techniques were still being used in parts of America up until the early twentieth century. Suicides were sometimes famously buried at a crossroads or with a stake in the grave to keep the restless soul from returning. But the most famous vampire event took place in New England during the 1890s. In quick succession a mother named Mary and her daughters Mary Olive and Mercy Brown died of tuberculosis. The family was sad, but then that sort of thing happened a lot. But when their son/brother got sick the neighbors jumped to the obvious conclusion that one of the deceased was a vampire and was making the poor boy ill. A mob exhumed all the bodies. While the Marys had started decomposing, Mercy still looked pretty good for a dead person. She had also shifted position, from her back to her side. Obviously, this meant that she was one of the walking dead, and not just that the gravediggers had jostled her coffin. Since she was clearly a vampire, her father cut out her heart, sliced it open, then burned it, mixed the ashes with water, and made his family members drink it so they would not get sick themselves. While it was probably less effective, this concoction almost certainly tasted better than liquid cold medicine. Historians believe that similar heart burnings were not uncommon in New England over a 150-year period in the eighteenth and nineteenth centuries. Those medieval Bulgarians are looking pretty damn advanced now, aren't they?

> According to most studies, people's number one fear is public speaking. Number two is death. . . . This means to the average person, if you go to a funeral, you're better off in the casket than doing the eulogy.
>
> Jerry Seinfeld, comedian

## BURN, BABY, BURN

Depending on where you live, burning bodies after death is either an ancient practice or a modern controversy. Either way, it is both one hell of a goodbye barbeque and a great way to ensure that the discount hospital your cheap family took you to diagnosed the whole "dead" thing correctly.

The number of cremations still varies widely from country to country, with 99 percent of all Japanese people choosing immolation after death while less than 10 percent of people in Poland do. The numbers make sense when you realize that cremation has a long history in the Eastern world, while in much of the Western world it was considered antireligious, heathen, and suspect until a criminal playing dress up on the run brought cremation to the forefront of European and American society. Doctor William Price brought the discussion to a head in 1884, because if anyone knew how to make calm, rational decisions about death, it was the Victorians.

Since 1968, cremations have outnumbered burials in the United Kingdom. But less than 100 years before, people didn't even know if burning a dead body was legal. Cremations had occurred in the UK before that year, but few had been widely publicized because Hallmark had yet to stock "We're Having a Cremation!" invitations. A crematorium was built in London in 1879, but public controversy prevented it from burning anything but a single horse for the next six years. Cremation societies were formed (because rich people in the 1800s were really, really bored) and tried to convince the country of the benefits of the practice, including the fact that gentile Victorian women would not suffer the indignity of their corpses being invaded by maggots and worms, something everyone agreed was seriously unladylike. But public opinion was against them. The mortuary profession in general made sure that cremation wasn't an acceptable option, and, knowing it would reduce their business, embalmers and casket makers embarked on a propaganda campaign of their own, probably using now-outdated slogans like "Don't be a Flamer."

Then along came the crazy Welshman. Dr. Price was a medical doctor by trade who believed in some of the most controversial political ideas of the day, including socialism, vegetarianism, free love, and expanding the right to vote to everyone (except women, obviously, because that would be insane). After fleeing Great Britain to avoid arrest he decided he would return to liberate the Welsh from their English rulers. The most logical way to do this, he felt, was to become a self-appointed Druid priest, complete with his own creative take on the "traditional" attire, including a fox fur hat, all green clothing, and a long beard. After all, nothing says "Please take me seriously" like dressing up as Santa Claus on laundry day. At the age of eighty-one Price fathered a child and named him Jesus Christ, proving celebrities have always given their kids weird names. Sadly, the boy died only five months later, and the doctor announced his intention to burn his son's body on a pyre.

The police were alerted when Dr. Price started cremating his son, and he was arrested and brought to trial. The judge ruled that while cremation was not socially acceptable, there was no actual law making it illegal, meaning you just probably wouldn't be invited to the best parties anymore if people found out. Under English common law this decision effectively legalized the practice. Price cremated his son, and slowly but surely others followed suit. While many Christian leaders raised objections in the UK and America, saying that there needed to be a complete body for Jesus to resurrect at the end times, others were more open-minded. Numerous bishops shut down the detractors by pointing out that surely a God that could raise bodies that had long ago turned to dust could raise ones more recently turned to ash, to which Dr. Price, if he had any sense of comedic irony, should have responded, "Ooooo, burn."

# INTERIOR DECORATING FOR THE CREEPY

There are two things college students do when they visit the Czech Republic while backpacking through Europe trying to "find themselves." One is hitting up Prague's amazing club scene and drinking some mind-bending absinthe, the other is visiting a tiny, out-of-the-way Catholic chapel. And if the tourists have the absinthe right before visiting the chapel, they may "find themselves" being confined to a mental institution when they start telling people about seeing skeletons climb the walls while they were there. Because, although on the outside the Sedlec Ossuary just looks like your average small church surrounded by a large cemetery, on the inside it is one of the most macabre buildings in the world.

It all started in 1278 when a monk came back from Jerusalem with a tiny sack full of dirt. He claimed it was from the hill where Jesus was crucified and proceeded to sprinkle it among the monastery's small cemetery, imbuing it with holy goodness. Overnight that bit of land became the most popular place to be buried in all of Central Europe. Thousands of families who would have buried their devout relatives in the Holy Land if it wasn't for that whole traveling-hundreds-of-miles-with-a-dead-body thing decided being buried in a place where some dust allegedly from a hill where Jesus might have stood more than 1,000 years ago was just as impressive. The cemetery was already starting to run out of room when the Black Death hit Europe. Suddenly bodies had to be buried half a dozen deep in order to fit everyone, resulting in a disturbing underground corpse orgy. Some of the oldest bodies were just dug up and replaced with newer ones, because once you are dead you can't really complain.

Once limbs started just poking out of the ground randomly the monks realized they had to do something about the room problem. They assigned one of their members to dig up even more of the graves and deposit the bones in the newly constructed ossuary. One would hope that the removal of so many bodies would be treated with respect but considering the monk selected for this job was half blind the remains were probably not removed with archaeological precision. In fact, the brother just threw all the bones into giant piles that reached to the ceiling.

> ***Using bones from more than 40,000 skeletons [František Rint] formed garlands of skulls, a giant coat of arms, even a chandelier made from at least one of every bone in the human body.***

In 1870 a wealthy family finally decided that something a little more respectful needed to be done with the remains. They hired a woodcarver named František Rint to arrange the bones in some sort of order. It turned out his version of "respectful" was pretty disturbing: Using bones from more than 40,000 skeletons he formed garlands of skulls, a giant coat of arms, even a chandelier made from at least one of every bone in the human body. While the result is one of the most surreal things you will ever see, with skulls staring at you from every angle, there is genuine artistry in the work. Rint obviously paid attention to the size and shape of not just the different types of bones, but each one's individual characteristics. For example, when making a bird in the coat of arms he used the hand of someone who suffered from severe arthritis, fusing many of the bones together. It sounds kind of beautiful until you remember it isn't actually a building material, it's some poor dead person's hand! Still, one historian referred to Rint as the "Michelangelo of bone art," so sorry, in case you were wondering, that nickname is already taken. It took Rint ten years to create his gothic masterpiece but he was so proud of the end result that he signed it—in bones, obviously. He was paid handsomely for his work. These days the tiny church is the most popular tourist attraction in the Czech Republic, drawing more than 200,000 slightly weird visitors a year.

# POSTMORTEM PHOTOGRAPHY

Saying the Victorians were obsessed with death is a bit like saying nerds like Star Wars. Their mourning rituals became almost as complex, expensive, and socially important as weddings—in some cases, even more so. Fortunately for these death-obsessed Goth wannabes, emerging technology meant they never had to go more than a few minutes without looking at a dead body.

For the middle classes, having a portrait painted of a loved one was prohibitively expensive, but as photography became more common it was much easier just to sit a few minutes for a picture rather than many hours for a painting. Photographs still weren't cheap though, and for many families the cost didn't seem like it was worth it, at least not until someone died. That's when they suddenly realized they would like to have an image to remember their relative by, money be damned. These days we would resign ourselves to the fact that it was too late, that photographing someone in their coffin is slightly creepy. The Victorians decided it was not only appropriate but beautiful—and hell, who even needs the coffin?

With this mindset photographing the dead became one of the biggest cultural fads of the century. In fact, over a sixty-year period starting around 1840, far more pictures were taken of the deceased than the living. And while Queen Victoria may have immortalized her beloved Albert in a marble bust that she included in most family portraits after his death, her less well-off subjects were forced to pose with the dead bodies themselves. While in many cases the dead were posed to look as if they were still alive, with their eyes propped open, or reclining as if they were sleeping, you can usually tell who the late family member is. At the time, sitting for a picture meant staying absolutely still for ten or fifteen minutes, similar to being in an MRI machine today. Any movement would render the final image blurry. The dead were, not surprisingly, very good at staying absolutely still and therefore were always the clearest individual in the final image, even if a body part fell off halfway through. People carried these photos around with them, wore them in lockets, and displayed them prominently in their houses. Fortunately, today photographing the dead is largely limited to war reporters, forensic scientists, and modern artists looking to cause a bit of controversy.

**DEATH IS JUST NATURE'S WAY OF TELLING YOU TO SLOW DOWN.**

DICK SHARPLES, WRITER

## STIFFS AND SCIENCE

For hundreds of years, doctors have been trying to get their hands on some grade-A corpses for medical study, and today you can sign up to have your body donated to science after death. Some people do it for the love of scientific advancement, some because the cost of a funeral is too prohibitive, and at least one well-muscled guy probably just wanted to see if he could impress some lady doctors after death.

But when the medical profession first started operating on cadavers, you couldn't just offer your body up to science. In fact, legally dead bodies couldn't even be operated on. Eventually the laws were changed so the bodies of criminals put to death were turned over to science, because, while normal people obviously deserved to go to the grave in one piece, no one really cared about criminals. In fact, this was considered an added punishment; convicts were more likely to work with the police, even knowing they would die anyway, if it meant they wouldn't be turned over for dissection.

As news spread that the inside of a human was really quite cool looking, people outside the medical profession started expressing their desire to spend a day watching someone pull out a serial killer's intestines. Eventually human dissections were huge draws, with tickets going for large amounts of money. Even women got in on the act, and for fun sometimes the doctor would invite women down from the audience to touch the corpse. See what people did for entertainment before television was invented?

But dissection was only one of the fun things you could do with dead criminals. Italian scientist Giovanni Aldini experimented with electricity and the human body, by which we mean he straight up electrocuted dead guys. Knowing this was far too entertaining to keep to himself, in 1803 he demonstrated his technique in front of an audience in London. Aldini applied electrodes to the face and limbs of George Foster, a man who had murdered his wife and child, and the killer's eyes opened and his muscles twitched. But Aldini wasn't finished yet. Since no one is really going to tell you you're going too far with the disrespect to a family annihilator's body, the scientist shoved an electrified rod up the cadaver's ass. People started freaking out when this caused Foster to sit up. Aldini became so famous for these bizarre spectacles that most historians think he inspired Mary Shelley's Frankenstein.

Eventually even the number of executed criminals weren't enough for the dissection-loving public and doctors. This led to not so much a "donation" policy as a "grave-robbing" policy. If your family didn't care enough to stand by your grave for a couple nights until your body started to decompose, there was a decent chance that someone would come along and dig you up. It was nothing personal; these thieves were even known to dig up their own family members and sell them if the price was right.

The most famous of these body snatchers were the Scottish duo William Burke and William Hare. They found all that digging to be rather inconvenient, however, and got around it by just straight-up murdering seventeen people and then selling their bodies. Once they were caught and the government realized exactly what lengths everyone was willing to go to in the name of science, the restrictions on cadaver usage were relaxed. That's why today you can help advance the future of medicine by donating your body. Just be aware that nothing ever changes: Even legitimate medical schools get into trouble to this day for making money by selling bits of the bodies they don't need.

## DEATH IS A HAIRY SITUATION

In August 2012, it was announced that the preserved corpse of Julia Pastrana would finally be given a proper burial, a mere 152 years after she died. While most people tend to bury their loved ones immediately after they leave this world, Julia's husband chose not to, for one very good—if also very sick—reason; she was worth a lot of money even if she was dead. These days celebrities' families make money after the deaths of their loved ones through their song catalogs (Elvis, Kurt Cobain) or by auctioning off their expensive jewelry (Elizabeth Taylor). But in the 1800s the loved ones of famous people could make money just by displaying the dearly departed's corpse. Although, to be fair, this would probably work today as well. They should have tried it with Michael Jackson; they barely would have had to embalm him.

Julia Pastrana was one of the world's most famous curiosities during her short lifetime. Born in Mexico, her mother sold her to Theodore Lent, who would become her manager and take her around the world under names like the Nondescript and the Ape Woman. Today we might call her hirsute: she was born with a layer of thick black hair covering her body that never went away. One of the most popular bearded ladies of her time, she also had unusually large ears, a thick nose, and a heavy jaw that, combined with her hairy coating, made her look a bit like a monkey. Despite this she was said to be extremely ladylike, with small hands and feet, and she always dressed in the most fashionable clothing, cinching her waist in a tiny corset.

Lent certainly found her attractive. He taught her to dance and read three different languages, eventually marrying her. Their marriage was not just a business arrangement either, as Julia soon fell pregnant. Unfortunately, her son died shortly after he was born and Julia followed four days later, aged just twenty-six. Her husband, while depressed, didn't want to lose his biggest money-maker. Their son had been born covered in hair as well, so Lent had both his son and Julia embalmed and started touring with his late family around Europe, where they remained as popular as ever. Thousands of people lined up wherever they went and paid up to the equivalent of three days' wages in order to see the hairy family. Even after Lent discovered and married another bearded lady he continued to display his late wife to huge crowds. Eventually Lent went insane and died in 1884.

Julia's body was hidden from the public until 1921 when it went on display in Norway. In the 1970s there was discussion of an American tour, which fortunately never happened. The body was stolen and went missing for eleven years before being recovered in 1990, but it wasn't until 2012 that someone pointed out maybe they should finally bury the poor woman and her child.

# SMELL GOOD OR DIE TRYING

The road to sainthood has never been easy, but at least it's specific: Live holy, die persecuted, and leave a pleasant-smelling corpse. That last one is key, because it turns out that even after living a life full of good deeds and devotion to the Almighty, possibly the most important step to becoming a saint is making sure everyone at the funeral gets a big ol' sniff of your rotting corpse and thinks, "Now *that* smells nice."

Smelling good is mentioned a few times in the Bible, most likely as a metaphor for being a good person, but in the Middle Ages the Catholic Church started taking the idea literally. Around this time, the men in charge of deciding who got to become a saint began taking into consideration accounts of the smell of the deceased. By 1758 the pope made it an official test of sainthood. Considering how rank day-to-day life was in that time due to a lack of basic hygiene, inadequate sewage, and the close proximity of farm animals, smelling good was obviously a miracle in life, let alone after death.

But even long before that, people knew the importance of holy people smelling amazing after they died, however that death might have come about. In A.D. 155, St. Polycarp was burned alive. Instead of giving off a slightly disturbing BBQ aroma, his devotees reported that he smelled like fragrant incense and, bizarrely, baking bread. Later, both Saint Thérèse de Lisieux and Saint Teresa of Avila were reported to have sent the smell of roses through their respective nunneries right at the moments of their deaths.

Sure, they could have achieved this by splashing on some really strong perfume when they felt their time was nigh, a sort of Eau de Holiness, if you will. But there may actually be a scientific explanation for this bizarre phenomenon. Many saints were slightly odd and starved themselves, and both anorexics and schizophrenics seem to smell better than other people when they die. Both conditions lead to an increase of ketones (a sugar produced by the body) throughout the body and after death the ketones break down, letting off a sickly sweet scent. That being said, in most cases historians think the followers of holy people just embalmed their bodies better than the average person, making their corpses noticeably fragrant.

But what if no one had been around to sniff you as you were burned, buried, or starved to death? Fortunately, all was not lost. Sometimes future saints only became popular long after they were dead and buried. In that case, they still had one more chance to prove they had died in the odor of sanctity; all it took was some seemingly well-intentioned people digging up their body or breaking into their tomb. St. Isidore reportedly still smelled lovely over 450 years after he had shuffled off this mortal coil. St. Dominic's fragrant scent was supposedly so powerful that it even emanated from his sealed tomb.

The main problem with smelling so nice was that the people who dug you up then tended to take bits of you home as relics. This was known to backfire on them, though; one saint's fecal matter was said to smell so enticing after he died that a woman smeared it on her face, only to discover too late that it had reverted to its more usual scent. Talk about a crappy day!

**I HAVE LOST FRIENDS, SOME BY DEATH—OTHERS BY SHEER INABILITY TO CROSS THE STREET.**

VIRGINIA WOOLF, AUTHOR (DIED 1941)

# THE NUMBER ONE POSTMORTEM BEAUTY TIP

The problem of rotting corpses is one every society has tried to deal with at some point, because, all differences aside, the smell of a decaying human body is something we can all agree is not pleasant. Some religions insist burials occur almost immediately so that the health risks pose the smallest problem. Other cultures have tried different ways to mask the smell or preserve the corpse over the days or weeks until it can be buried. Some of these attempts, like mummification, did not allow for viewing the unspoiled body one last time. As open-casket funerals became the norm in Western society, it became more important to find an effective way to keep the dead both pretty and sanitary. Strangely, the man who finally developed the embalming process undertakers still use today did it for completely selfish reasons.

Thomas Holmes was in medical school in the 1840s and had dissected his fair share of cadavers. However, the best ways of preserving bodies at that time (large amounts of arsenic and mercury) also happened to be hazardous to the medical students. As if cutting into dead people wasn't bad enough, the aspiring doctors did it knowing that the toxins could put them on that slab themselves any day now. Holmes knew there had to be a better way. Borrowing from other French and American doctors' work, he perfected his technique shortly before the start of the Civil War. His timing was perfect.

During the war it was vital that bodies be effectively preserved before their long train trips home from the battlefields, otherwise the living passengers started to complain about the stench coming from the baggage cars. It also had to be done fast and in huge numbers. By the end of the war some 40,000 fallen soldiers had been embalmed, 10 percent of them by Holmes himself, at the then exorbitant price of $25–$100 apiece. The doctor made his name when he embalmed Colonel Elmer Ellsworth, the first famous casualty of the war. The young colonel's body was laid out for viewing in the capital, and the press commented on the pleasant effect of the embalming. Apparently it was a slow news day.

> ***By the end of the war some 40,000 fallen soldiers had been embalmed, 10 percent of them by Dr. Holmes himself, at the then exorbitant price of $25–$100 apiece.***

Dr. Holmes became the go-to person for embalming. After the war he was rumored to have collected some of his best specimens and kept them around his home. While slightly morbid, it was no different from any other artist being proud of his work, if said work was set on a couch and stared unseeingly at you when you came for a visit.

Of course, embalming only went so far toward making a corpse riddled with bullet holes pretty, so the first official society of morticians was also formed during the war. But it was the assassination of Abraham Lincoln that really made embalming a funeral necessity. As his preserved corpse traveled back to Illinois from Washington, D.C., thousands turned out to see it and were impressed by how good the late president looked compared to their own deceased relatives. Soon, people were clamoring to disguise the ravages of death with embalming. Schools for embalmers opened in the 1880s, and by the turn of the century most states regulated the practice. However, fly-by-night embalmers must have been a real problem, considering most states didn't even bother making attending elementary school compulsory until almost twenty years later.

# THE FIRST MAUSOLEUM

In 353 B.C., Mausolus, a sort of governor for the Persian Empire who controlled a small area in present-day Turkey, died. His wife Artemisia (who also happened to be his sister; things were different back then) was distraught. Since she and her husband had been crazy about building temples when he was alive, she decided the most fitting tribute for him was to build a temple-like building for his ashes, which, of course, makes sense in the same way that if you really like hamburgers, your tomb should logically look like a McDonald's. The resulting temple wasn't the first aboveground structure to house the remains of an important person, but it was so over the top and iconic that it gave us the word *mausoleum*.

Money was no object for Artemisia. She was so in love with her husband-brother that legend has it that she mixed some of his ashes with wine and drank them—and if she was willing to down a mixed drink that disgusting you know she cared enough to give him the best tomb in history. Artemisia asked around for the best craftsmen, eventually employing hundreds of them, including the four most famous Greek sculptors of the day, who were hired to make dozens of statues. Unfortunately for Artemisia, she died only two years into the project, well before it was finished. Since the plans were already finalized, and since the tomb was set to be a real resume booster, the workers kept building.

In the end the mausoleum stood 145 feet high, topped with a bronze statue of a chariot drawn by four horses. It was surrounded by thirty-six columns with a statue in between each pair. The walls were covered in great friezes of mythical battles. Huge sections were made of solid marble. In short, it was exactly the sort of tomb you would expect for a man so important that you'd never even heard of him until two minutes ago. But the finished product was so impressive it became one of the Seven Wonders of the Ancient World.

Like most of these wonders, it doesn't exist today. Sometime before A.D. 1404, various earthquakes reduced most of the tomb to rubble. Knights from Western Europe on their way to the Holy Land then used that rubble to fortify their castles. What marble they didn't use as building blocks they melted down to collect lime. Grave robbers broke into the sealed tomb and took any treasures that might have been in there. And because people didn't have historic conservation societies back then, as late as the 1850s the conveniently precut ancient marble blocks were being shipped around the Mediterranean as building supplies, adding a bit of class to docks and fortresses as far away as Malta.

If you can't make it to Turkey to check out the ruins, there are plenty of other places to be inspired by this historic tomb. Most of the good remaining statues from the site were, of course, taken by the English and now reside in the British Museum. Even the countries that didn't manage to steal the actual artifacts had no qualms about stealing the designs. At least nine modern buildings were heavily inspired by the mausoleum's architecture, including the Los Angeles City Hall, Grant's Tomb, the Masonic Temple in Washington, D.C., and the Shrine of Remembrance in Australia. The takeaway point here is that architects apparently believe that if it ain't broke, don't fix it.

**DYING IS EASY.
COMEDY IS DIFFICULT.**

EDMUND GWENN, ACTOR (DIED 1959)

# SELF-MUMMIFICATION

The process of preparing a dead body, be it by embalming, mummifying, or a variety of other ways, is a time-consuming and often expensive process. However, a small group of Buddhist monks in northern Japan got around that postmortem work by getting themselves all ready for a pretty death before they died.

Called Sokushinbutsu, or self-mummification, the procedure was so difficult that while hundreds of monks are believed to have attempted it, fewer than two dozen are known to have succeeded. The process took years and was so unpleasant it is amazing anyone got through it at all. First the monk had to get rid of all his body fat by eating only low- and nonfat foods like nuts and seeds, since fat does not fare so well after death. While this terrible diet would make anyone lethargic, the monk also combined it with an extreme exercise regime, just to make sure any extra fat was burned off. After almost three years of that regime, for the next 1,000 days he managed to make his diet even worse, giving up nuts for bark and roots. When he was thirsty he washed it down with tea made from a poisonous sap. To get an idea of what that was doing to his insides, the sap was normally used to lacquer pottery. It wasn't pleasant, but that wasn't the point, in fact any vomiting was seen as a good thing. The sap also provided the added bonus of making the body so polluted with poison that even maggots would know to stay away, thus preserving the body in death. Here's a tip: if even maggots think it's a bad idea, it is a really bad idea.

***Here's a tip: if even maggots think it's a bad idea, it is a really bad idea.***

After five and a half years of this self-inflicted torture, the monk was ready to die. He sat down in a tiny stone tomb and waited to starve to death. The only thing in the tomb with him was a string, at the other end of which was a bell. Every day (although how he measured time accurately is a mystery) he would ring the bell letting his less-dedicated but much saner brothers know he was still alive. When the bell stopped ringing the small hole was sealed. One thousand days later, the monks opened the tomb. Almost all of the time there was just a rotting body left, but the monk would still be venerated for at least giving it the old college try. If the dead monk had managed to mummify himself correctly he was believed to have achieved enlightenment. To inspire those around them the preserved bodies were put on display in the temples, because nothing says, "The years of torture are totally worth it" like a slowly crumbling mummified body.

You can still go today and see sixteen of these Buddhist mummies. And while the practice has been outlawed in Japan since the 1800s, and officially is not sanctioned by the Buddhist religion, there are rumors that it still happens today. Some people never learn.

# SUTTEE IS SUCKY

One funeral custom that was almost certainly not thought up by women was the ancient custom of suttee, or sati, most famously practiced in India. It involved the widow of a dead man voluntarily lying down on his funeral pyre and being burned alive. No one is exactly sure when this funeral immolation first started, but some estimate it at around 5,500 years old. The first documented case occurred in 908 B.C., long before women had fought for the right to say, "Are you freaking kidding me?"

There are various theories as to why this disturbing act became popular in the first place. One theory is that, by killing herself, the wife could cleanse her husband's sins, ensuring he had a good time in the afterlife. The ancient Greeks theorized that there was a much more earthly reason for the practice: at a time when old men were routinely married to very young girls, the knowledge that their life depended on their wrinkly husband staying alive made wives more likely to take care of the men and less likely to poison them so they could marry someone younger. Suttee also served to dispose of any surplus women in a tribe, ensuring they would not look outside their own people for a husband. You can see why looking around might be an appealing prospect, especially if those other tribes wouldn't make them commit suicide when their husband died.

While ostensibly voluntary, the pressure to lie down on her husband's funeral pyre was intense. There are recorded instances of widows quite understandably changing their minds at the last minute and running off, only to be brought back at knifepoint. Others were drugged or even tied down, calling into question the whole "voluntary" part. While the lives of women in medieval India, especially lower-caste women, were not great, women who committed suttee guaranteed that they would be revered as goddesses. The goddess powers apparently came even before their death, since it was maintained that the widow felt no pain as she was burned alive. Although, assuredly, no men tried it out first just to make sure that theory was correct.

Suttee was regulated as early as the 1200s, but how many funerals followed the regulations is unknown. First the widow had to assure the government that she was totally serious about wanting to be burned alive, just to make sure no one was forcing her. (Oh, the guy standing behind her with the sword? Just ignore him. He's a family friend, nothing to worry about.) By the 1500s she was required to get permission from the police, who would offer her gifts to change her mind and try to delay the event as long as possible if she would not. When the British took over they had a relatively relaxed view of suttee, regarding it as a local custom and probably no more painful than a really hot curry. But once word got back to London about what was going on in their colony, pressure was put upon the Raj to end the practice. It was banned by the British government in 1829, but the practice continued. In 1987, the Indian government again banned suttee, although sometimes they just can't keep some of those widows from jumping in that fire, as rare instances continue to occur to this day.

**Arthur hoped and prayed that there wasn't an afterlife. Then he realized there was a contradiction there and merely hoped that there wasn't an afterlife.**

Douglas Adams, author (died 2001)

## HANGING AROUND AFTER DEATH

Around 700 B.C., the Bo people in southern China decided the best thing to do with their dead was to raise them up to the heavens, literally. The Bo people lived in the mountains and apparently placed a religious significance on the highest points, which may have represented calm and serenity in an otherwise calamitous life full of wars and natural disasters. After all, it's hard to have a battle right on top of a mountain. So when you died, if your family really loved you, they made sure you went as high up the mountain cliffs as possible. They accomplished this by dangling bodies hundreds of feet in the air, until the hills were alive with—well, the dead. And so was born one of the most labor-intensive funeral services of all time.

The first step in the process was for your family to make you a coffin, although some experts think it was important to make your own before you died, because while your family loved you enough to haul your corpse up a mountain, the arm cramps and blisters resulting from building your coffin was going too far. After all, it was carved out of a single piece of wood and took a long time. Once the coffin was ready, the body was placed inside, along with the necessary tools for the afterlife. Like the Egyptians, allowing their dead to take stuff along on the journey seems to have been important, as one coffin examined in 1974 contained twenty-nine shirts and thirteen pairs of pants. It is not recorded if the Bo thought the afterlife was going to lack laundry facilities. Finally, it was time to take the full coffin and place it as far up the cliff as they could. Some families obviously loved their relatives more than others, as the heights vary from 10 to 150 yards off the ground on the vertical cliff faces.

***The biggest mystery surrounding this special funeral ritual is how exactly the deceased's relatives got the coffins on the cliffs in the first place.***

The biggest mystery surrounding this special funeral ritual is how exactly the deceased's relatives got the coffins on the cliffs in the first place. The solid wood, combined with the body, could weigh in at over 550 pounds. Considering the height and sheerness of the cliffs, if the people placing the coffins were not careful, deaths and funerals could become a never-ending loop. There are three theories. One is that earth ramps might have been used, but this would have been difficult with such a small population. The second involves building primitive scaffolding, but there is no actual physical evidence for this. The most accepted theory is that ropes were used to lower the coffins down the cliff, but this doesn't account for the drastic height differences between resting places—unless the cords often slipped and the resulting rope burn made the family unwilling to haul the coffin back up.

These days, the cliffs with the hanging coffins are popular hiking destinations for tourists. But, if you ever find yourself trekking through southern China, try to remember what hundreds of years of wind and wet do to exposed wood: the heavy, decaying coffins have been known to plunge several hundred feet to the hiking trails below. It became a serious enough problem that the Chinese government has launched maintenance work to stabilize the sites three times since 1974.

Now, if you do find yourself up close and personal with one of these ancient coffins, try to be polite. The areas they are found in are unregulated, and grave robbing by tourists is a problem. Apparently there is a certain type of person who is more interested in bringing home an ancient finger bone as a souvenir than an adorable stuffed panda.

# FUNERARY CANNIBALISM

When a relative dies, your first response probably isn't, "My, don't they look delicious." At least we hope not. But while cannibalism is distasteful to our modern sensibilities, tribes all over the world once engaged in this practice. And while eating parts of conquered enemies was most common, funerary cannibalism, the practice of eating friends and relatives, also seems to have been normal. The oldest evidence we have of preparing a meal out of a dead relative comes from the Iron Age, but in modern times cannibalism was routine among some isolated populations until the 1950s and '60s. Of course, thanks to the new craze of smoking bath salts, it's seeing a comeback today as well.

The Wari' are an indigenous Brazilian people who eat their own tribe members. There are strict rules around who gets to eat whom though, and it's important to get it right. When a person dies, their relatives in the surrounding villages are informed, and they then travel to the deceased's village for the funeral. Since this usually takes a few days (the postal service and public transport being notoriously unreliable no matter what your community's version of it is) and the Amazon does not have the ideal climate for preserving flesh, by the time friends and family get around to eating the deceased person, the corpse is usually bloated and rotting. This is a good thing, however. It is considered inappropriate to seem like you are enjoying eating your dead relative, or eating too quickly, so the less palatable their roasted flesh the better. Fortunately it is only the more distant relatives who are expected to partake in the feast; immediate family is excused because eating your mom is a bit too weird even for cannibals. Children and the elderly were often given the tastiest bits, which include the liver and brain. The idea behind eating a loved one is that part of the person would continue on in the world, even if that world mainly involves the small intestine and eventually a toilet.

***There are strict rules around who gets to eat whom though, and it's important to get it right.***

The Fore people of Australia also practiced mortuary cannibalism until the government put a stop to it around sixty years ago, and it was the job of the female relatives to prepare the body of the deceased. You were allowed different bits of the body depending on your relation to the corpse; the men, for example, were usually given the red meat from the legs, while the women had to make do with the stuff that probably would have been better made into sausage. Unfortunately, around 1900 a member of the tribe seems to have developed a previously unknown disease called Kuru, similar to mad cow disease. When he died and was eaten, the disease infected others. Eventually, Kuru became an epidemic among the Fore people. They still ate their dead, of course, but the added sense of danger probably made for an interesting seasoning.

The Yanomamo people of Venezuela also ate their dead, but in a less literal way. Rather than eating the flesh, they would grind up the bones into a powder, mix them with a banana paste, and eat them like a smoothie. In some cases the ashes of a cremated body may be consumed as well.

At least one modern sect is rumored to still practice cannibalism today. India's Aghori holy men have been filmed fishing bodies out of the Ganges and consuming small parts of them. The river is considered holy, and by eating bodies that have been in it the men hope to gain special powers, including levitation and control over the weather. If they are right, the answer to global warming might lie with a few hundred Indian cannibals, which is almost certainly something no one has brought up at a climate summit yet.

# MORTAL COMBAT

Ancient peoples didn't like the idea of a loved one going to the afterlife all alone and they decided that it was so much easier when you brought a friend along. So, when an important person died, the community made sure someone else went with him, whether it was a wife or slave or just a random prisoner. But, at some point, one of these peoples, most likely the Etruscans or ancient Greeks, decided that slitting the throat of a slave did not make for the most interesting sendoff. Adding a competitive element would really help put the "fun" back in funeral—and so the gladiator was born. These gladiators were called Bustuarii after the *bustum*, the tomb or funeral mound of the deceased.

> ***Adding a competitive element would really help put the "fun" back in funeral—and so the gladiator was born.***

At the time, the Greeks and Etruscans just grabbed two slaves, gave them some swords, and told them to fight to the death. There wasn't any body armor and training was minimal, giving the events much more of a Three Stooges sort of feel than one might expect from funeral entertainment. But this was okay because the main goal still wasn't excitement, it was for someone to die; the blood spilled was an offering that would make the gods and the dead person happy. But by the time the Roman's borrowed the idea, it had gotten a bit more complex.

The first recorded Roman gladiator match was in 264 B.C. at the funeral of Brutus, a distant relative of the more famous assassin of Julius Caesar. This funeral was not a private affair. His sons chose six prisoners to fight in Rome's cattle market while the public watched. And less than fifty years later one day of mortal combat wasn't enough for a family to honor a particularly important man; Consul Marcus Aemilius's funeral gladiator games lasted three days and included twenty-two men. Apparently being accompanied to the afterlife by almost two dozen very angry men who had died because of you was still preferable to going solo . . .

The spectacle continued to grow and, by 175 B.C., hundreds of gladiators were involved in weeklong festivities that included huge feasts. Some particularly classy funerals had musicians play music to keep up the pace of the fights, making them literal dances of death. Eventually these festivities were so expected when saying goodbye to family or friends that men and women alike left money in their will specifically to pay for the gladiators. Even the less well-off had smaller fights to the death during their own sendoffs, with the goal of keeping up with the Juliuses. (It's like keeping up with the Joneses, but with more togas and fewer Cadillacs.) The idea was to outdo all other previous funeral fights so that yours, and therefore you, would be talked about forever. The brinkmanship backfired though, and chroniclers and historians eventually became so bored by the repetitive festivities that they stopped noting the largest ones in their histories. Just something to keep in mind for anyone who thought this would be a great way to get their fifteen minutes of fame.

Then in 105 B.C. the first ever gladiator match sans funeral was held. Almost overnight these fights became public spectacles tied more to politics than funerals. Since the spilling of blood to cleanse the soul of the dead was no longer necessary, the fights became about training and skill, rather than simply fights to the death. Fortunately for the bloodthirsty Coliseum spectators, Christians and lions showed up just in time to replace the gladiators when it came to no-win death matches.

# CAN'T TOUCH THIS

Ever since humankind started burying folks in well-defined graves, people have been worried about their bodies being moved from those same graves. History has shown that the idea of a "final" resting place was little more than a nice lie people told themselves during a difficult time. In reality grave robbers, body snatchers, and limited space meant that after a decent interval had passed (and everyone who would care had died) the fight for the space where a person was buried became a free-for-all. But some soon-to-be corpses weren't leaving their eternal rest to chance, and grave curses were born. It turns out that threatening anyone who disturbs your grave with a terrible death, makes them a bit less likely to move you.

The Egyptians are the most famous for these tomb curses. The curse of Tutankhamen was said to have killed dozens of the people who excavated his tomb, as well as their friends, families, and even pets. Nothing was safe from King Tut's horrible curse. The only problem with his curse is that he didn't actually leave one. While there are lots of lovely hieroglyphics around Tutankhamen's tomb, none of them even hint at death stalking anyone who disturbs it.

***The Egyptians are the most famous for these tomb curses. The curse of Tutankhamen was said to have killed dozens of the people who excavated his tomb, as well as their friends, families, and even pets.***

Other Egyptian pharaohs did leave curses though. While you may think of grave robbers as being the main looters of tombs, pharaoh Ankhtifi knew who the real threat was—his successors. His tomb included a curse on any future ruler who tried to take his resting place over for his own sarcophagus, promising that the gods would be pissed. Another pharaoh, Khentika Ikhekhi, made sure anyone who even entered the tomb knew they were screwed, and the king promised to "seize his neck like a bird."

While some Greek and Roman tombs also included curses, the habit mostly died out by the end of ancient times. The most famous modern grave curse is that of William Shakespeare. A poem the Bard himself penned adorns his grave, warning:

*Good friend, for Jesus' sake, forbear*
*To dig the dust enclosed here;*
*Blest be the man that spares these stones*
*And curst be that moves my bones.*

While the playwright almost certainly wrote this just to ensure that when the churchyard filled up his body would stay put, the threat worked. Even when the grave needed a renovation in 2008, the men in charge were told in no uncertain terms not to disturb the Bard's remains.

## DOES THIS MASK MAKE ME LOOK DEAD?

Throughout history the faces of dead people have fascinated societies. And since you can't sit and stare at a dead body all day, some of them found a way to keep those faces with the living in a (slightly) less creepy way. Death masks started as sculptural representations in ancient times, but by the 1700s, important people were having plaster poured right on their recently deceased faces. The French government even hired Madame Tussaud to make detailed casts of guillotined heads.

Death masks did have some altruistic reasons behind them. Before photography, some unclaimed corpses had death masks made of them so that if anyone came looking for a lost relative long after the body was in the ground they could be recognized, since skeletons tend to look a lot alike. One of these unknown dead washed up on the bank of the River Seine in Paris in the 1880s. The young girl was so beautiful even in death that her mask was given special attention and took hours longer than normal to make. She became known as L'Inconnue de la Seine, and her visage was so popular that rich Parisians had copies made and displayed in their houses. Even almost a century later her face was still a common sight; the first ever CPR mannequin, "Resusci Anne," first developed in the 1960s, was modeled after the long-dead girl's face. In case CPR training wasn't hard enough, just remember you're basically making out with a sixteen-year-old dead French girl.

***Even almost a century later her face was still a common sight; the first ever CPR mannequin, "Resusci Anne," first developed in the 1960s, was modeled after the long-dead girl's face.***

Mostly though, people made death masks because they liked creepy things. While the masks may have started out as almost exclusively for kings and other famous people, by the 1800s the most likely recipients of a postmortem facial were criminals. Some scientists and law enforcement officers claimed this was so the heads of bad men and women could be studied after death by experts in the popular pseudoscience phrenology, but really it was so the masks could be displayed and the surprisingly disturbed public would pay to come see them. Thus, the Scottish body snatcher William Burke's death mask was made shortly after his hanging in 1829, and more than 100 years later the people of Chicago were still turning out in droves to see the death masks of mobsters John Dillinger and Baby Face Nelson. When Bartolomeo Vanzetti and Nicola Sacco, anarchists convicted of murder in a very controversial trial during the 1920s, were executed their death masks weren't left up to just any guy who knew his way around plaster; William Gropper, a famous and controversial artist, was hired to get their faces just right for a fascinated public.

While we may not commemorate the dead's faces with masks anymore, that doesn't mean modern individuals find them any less fascinating. The aforementioned John Dillinger mask was sold at auction in 1991 for $10,000.

# THE ORIGINAL FRANKENSTEIN'S MONSTERS

One of the earlier forms of death ritual involved mummifying the bodies of the dead. In the same way that embalming allows us to believe that somehow death doesn't actually change anything, mummification made it easier for ancient peoples to be in the same room with week-old corpses for more than a few minutes.

The Egyptians are obviously the most famous mummifying civilization. While you may tend to think of pharaohs when you think of mummies, they were not the only members of Egyptian society to go through the process. Anyone who could afford it would expect the procedure after death. When the French and English invaded Egypt in the 1800s they found so many mummies that some were shipped back to Europe where aristocrats had "mummy unwrapping parties"—because nothing helps settle your stomach after a fancy dinner like a dried-out body.

While the Egyptians seem to have perfected the classic bandage mummification procedure rather quickly, the original mummifiers took a couple thousand years to figure it out. Four millennia before the first Egyptian mummy was made, the Chinchorro people in South America pioneered the technique. And while their attempts worked well enough that we still have examples of their mummies today, their process was even grosser than pulling brains out through the nose of the deceased as the Egyptians did.

The problem was that mummifying a body in one piece is really difficult. So from about 5000 to 3000 B.C., corpses were dismembered and each piece preserved individually before being put back together. This Frankenstein process was called the Black Mummy technique and started when all the skin was removed from the body. The skin was then taken away and tanned, often being divided into multiple pieces in the process. The head, arms, and legs were removed from the torso and each section had the muscles removed from the bone. After every part of the body was dried they were pieced back together, with stuffing made from plants to make the now shrunken body look more lifelike (plastic surgeons take note). The skin was reapplied and any spots it didn't cover were replaced with seal skin. A short black wig finished off the look (a later mummification development was the addition of a hat, which really tied the whole look together).

And your position in society or how much money you had when you died didn't matter. The Chinchorro mummified every member of their tribe who passed away. Women, children, old people, even miscarried fetuses—no matter, you were taken apart piece by piece when you kicked the bucket. Historians don't know why they went to all this effort, but it may have been for easier transportation of the bodies or as part of an ancestor cult. An awfully complicated way to pass the time—just like a movie star in makeup, perhaps the best analogy? Either way, sounds like an awfully complicated way to pass the time.

# DEATH AROUND THE WORLD

When people talk about our multicultural society and the importance of being culturally diverse, the first thing that leaps to mind probably isn't learning to respect how other cultures deal with corpses (most likely because if your go-to thought on anything involves dead bodies you will eventually be locked up). But societies around the world have all come up with different ways to dispose of their dead, taking into consideration their own specific historical, religious, and environmental challenges. Basically, if it involves a dead body it is best to let people go about their business, even if (or especially if) that includes involving strippers, vultures, or the music of Queen in the proceedings. What's really most important is finding common ground, and if there is one thing most societies around the world agree on when it comes to funerals it is this: there needs to be plenty of booze involved to take the edge off.

# SUPERSTITIONS FROM SIX FEET UNDER

There are literally thousands of superstitions surrounding death and burial. Every culture has its own, and frustratingly many contradict each other, so you better hope your people are practicing the correct ones. While humans are naturally superstitious, death makes us go right off the deep end with ways to reassure us that the Grim Reaper isn't coming for us as well.

## KEEP YOUR EYES ON THE PRIZE

To start, in order to keep yourself alive, never look the corpse in the eye. This is why—other than the fact that a dead stare is really creepy—most cultures would try to close the deceased eyes immediately, and if necessary would hold their eyelids down with coins or other objects. Even if you manage to get the corpse in the ground without looking in its eyes, the deceased's is always looking to come back and take someone with them to the great beyond, so be sure to come home from a funeral by a different route than the one you took to get there, or they will follow you.

## EAST AND WEST

Direction is everything when it comes to a corpse. One should always be carried around feet first. This was probably just because people in a deep sleep complained after being woken up by their head slamming against a door. When it comes to the burial, bury the body with its head in the west and its feet toward the east. If you live in a Christian country most of your cemeteries are mapped out this way to ensure that when Jesus comes back and all the corpses rise up they are facing the right direction. Of course, you could always just bury your loved ones with a compass. If you think the deceased was a good person, try to get them buried in the southern part of the graveyard. Historically that was where the best people were laid to rest, while everyone else got stuck at the north end, eternally sitting in the equivalent of coach while the better sort of corpses down south dine on the greener grass and fatter maggots.

### MAKE IT CLEAR

It's important not to confuse a dead person's soul as well. Open all the doors and windows to allow it easy access to the outside, since apparently souls can't just float through the ceiling. They are also either pretty dumb or very vain, and mirrors can confuse them, so be sure to turn all those around to face the wall.

### WEAR HAND-ME-DOWNS

Clothes are obviously important to the dead. While you can get all decked out for a wedding, it is vital you never wear anything brand-new to a funeral, especially shoes. You also never want to give a dead person your hand-me-downs. First of all, it would be mortifying if they looked better in your clothes than you did, but more importantly you would get unwell as the clothes rotted underground, and then you would die yourself due to quantum entanglement of you and your now corpse-filled clothes.

With all the precautions needed on top of funeral preparations, your loved ones turn out to be a lot more difficult in death than in life. Still, it's worth it if it means they don't take you with them.

**I WANT TO DIE LIKE MY FATHER, PEACEFULLY IN HIS SLEEP, NOT SCREAMING AND TERRIFIED, LIKE HIS PASSENGERS.**

Bob Monkhouse, comedian (died 2003)

# I'M TOO SEXY FOR THIS COFFIN

Some people find they have the time or inclination to plan their funerals down to the last detail. For someone with a terminal disease this can be a way of negating a feeling of powerlessness over death. Or, for control freaks with too much time on their hands, it can be a way to make sure they micromanage everything until the very end—and beyond. And since a significant portion of the human race has a sick sense of humor, one of the many things people decide they want at their funeral is completely inappropriate songs.

Funeral music started out as chants, usually as ways to drive off or appease spirits. But eventually this developed into actual songs. Different regions of the world had different types of traditional music played at funerals, but as time went on popular hits took the place of bagpipes and Dixieland jazz. In 2008, a cemetery in Australia released a list of the most commonly requested "weird" funeral songs:

- "The Show Must Go On" (Queen)
- "Stairway to Heaven" (Led Zeppelin)
- "Highway to Hell" (AC/DC)
- "Another One Bites the Dust" (Queen)
- "I'll Sleep When I'm Dead" (Bon Jovi)
- "Always Look on the Bright Side of Life" (Monty Python)
- "Ding-Dong! The Witch Is Dead" (The Wizard of Oz)
- "Hit the Road Jack" (Willie Nelson)
- "I'm Too Sexy" (Right Said Fred)
- Australian Football League club songs

But perhaps the living are partly to blame for these songs as well. Because while it's nice to honor the final wishes of the dead, at the end of the day what are they going to do, haunt you? Actually, if they are going to do that maybe it is best to give them what they want, even if it is completely inappropriate. But legally there are very few places in the world where the next of kin have to do anything the deceased asked for. This isn't just limited to small things like the crazy funeral music but includes how and where they want their remains laid to rest. So really, if you do find yourself faced with the possibility of "It's Raining Men" by the Weather Girls at your lecherous grandfather's funeral, rest easy that the law is on your side if you decide to skip that bit.

# ONE LAST JOYRIDE

Dead bodies are heavy. Not because they actually weigh any more than alive bodies, but they are notoriously selfish about sharing the load. So people figured out pretty quickly that getting them to their gravesites through other means than just carrying them was probably a good idea. Enter the hearse.

For hundreds of years the hearse consisted of a cart pulled by horses, the only difference between the cart taking the rich or the poor to the grave was being how fancy they were. The first hearses to ditch the horses actually used electric engines, but the French started using automobiles in 1907, an advance so shocking it was covered in *Scientific American* magazine. Then in 1909 H. D. Ludlow, an American funeral director on the cutting edge of technology, had his mechanic put together a weird combination of a bus and a horse-drawn hearse outfitted with an internal combustion engine. He used it at the funeral of a rich local man named Wilfrid A. Pruyn and soon all his richest customers were clamoring to take their last ride in this expensive car. By the 1920s the horse carts had gone the way of the dodo, and a decade later the hearse style we are familiar with today was standardized.

Hearses are special among funeral paraphernalia in that they can be kept or resold. While coffins go into the ground and flowers crumble eventually, the hearse can last for decades. The Cadillac that carried President Kennedy's casket from the hospital to Love Field in Dallas, Texas, was auctioned off in 2012. Because of its part in such a historic moment, most people, including the auctioneer, thought it would go for more than $1 million. Perhaps the creepiness factor was too much for car enthusiasts, because the final price was just $166,000.

One hearse that did sell was Elvis's. The Houston Brothers company bought the car from the original owners in the early

1980s. The company specialized in renting out hearses and, by all accounts, the Elvis connection made this hearse their most precious. Then in 1984 the owner had his son drive it to Miami from Georgia. Along the way the hearse ran out of gas and the young man, then only twenty-one, walked 4 miles to buy more. Remember how Elvis died on the toilet from overeating? Well, his hearse was about to meet a similar fate. While refilling the tank something went wrong, and when the owner's son took to the highway again the engine caught fire. He had no choice but to sit there and watch as this great piece of Elvis memorabilia burned up.

One hearse that never had a famous passenger is the one outside the Haunted Mansion in Disneyland. This is a hearse of the horse-drawn variety, and it first appeared in 1995. Shortly thereafter a rumor started that this was the hearse that had carried Mormon leader Brigham Young's body during his funeral. As myths go, this one is pretty easy to debunk, since there wasn't a hearse of any kind at Young's funeral. Way to go Disneyland, distorting reality as always.

# FUNERAL FASHION

More than any other social event, funerals have always had a strict dress code that people were expected to follow. However, just what that code entails has changed over the years and has depended a great deal on where you live.

Originally, white was a more common color for mourning, and it is still the standard funeral color in many Asian countries. In some cases only the upper classes or those closest to the deceased wore all white to express their sorrow, and, by the Renaissance, most countries in Europe had settled on black as the appropriate color for funerals.

While people would often wear mourning colors for a long time after the funeral of a spouse or child—in some cases for the rest of their lives—it was the Victorians who laid down a specific code for exactly when people could start dressing normally again. There were three stages to mourning a loved one:

- Full mourning
- Second mourning
- Half mourning

If your husband died, it would take three to four years to finish all of the stages, but if an uncle died, you might get to skip the preamble and start out at the last one. Servants got away with black armbands when one of their employers died. And just like in everything else, as always, men had more say in what colors they wore and when they wore them during their bereavement.

Widows had it the hardest. Not only had they just lost their husband and, in most cases, the source of their income, but they had to make themselves completely unattractive for years. Dresses that were required to be worn during full mourning were made out of dull black fabrics, no jewelry could be worn, and toning down the décolletage was expected. The most important part of the outfit for a widow in full mourning was a thick black veil that covered her face. After all, even a year after the fact she was probably still crying over her husband every day and nobody needs to see that. Obviously. Of course, since she wasn't supposed to leave the house for anything but church or the most vital errands anyway, no one would see her in the first place. The goal here was to make the widow completely unsexy. While she might be a great catch, her husband's friends were just going to have to wait until she got to wear colors again to hit on her.

Second mourning lasted up to a year and allowed the addition of—wait for it!—lavender trims and simple black jewelry. Finally half mourning allowed for some colorful trim and basic jewelry. But some women never left mourning, the most famous being Queen Victoria, who stayed in "widow's weeds" for forty years after her husband died. The style was catching, since her eldest daughter did the same thing after losing her husband. Eventually you couldn't move for black clad widows.

# BODY EXPOSURE

The Aboriginal tribes of Australia were never a truly homogenous group; some tribes buried their dead, others placed them in hollowed-out trees as sort of standup coffins. In certain areas a stranger or baby would have their corpse placed in a termite mound so the body would be disposed of quickly (hey, it's better than using a dingo!). And on some of the Australian islands people would bury their dead at sea. But perhaps the oddest—and one of the overwhelmingly popular—ways of disposing of dead bodies in the northern parts of the country, was body exposure.

In the first stage of body exposure the bodies are left exposed to the elements, on large wooden platforms. To keep the rotting process from being a bit too obvious, the corpse is covered with leaves. The bodies are left there for months, until the flesh falls off the bones. Once the body is reduced to a skeleton, the relatives take the bones back home. Souvenirs!

Since plain white bones are kind of boring to look at, relatives decorate them and paint the different bits, usually in a deep red color. The designs turn out so nice the bones are then used to decorate the house. The smaller bones might be turned into jewelry or simply carried around in a sack for years. In fact, colonists who befriended the natives when they arrived in Australia record widows showing up for lunch with large bags full of their late husband's remains tied around their necks. Mothers often did this with the bones of their children as well, in the hope that they would be reborn. One particular tribe in Queensland would tie skulls to tree trunks during celebrations so the dead could "see" the dances.

Some aboriginals faced a simpler form of body exposure when they died, as a type of punishment. When men died in battle they would be left where they fell, with weapons still stuck in them, so that others would know how they died and not to mess with the local tribe. Executed criminals were also left to the elements without the spiritual benefit of any funeral rituals. However, these simpler types of body exposure were not always a punishment. For some tribes, the normal way of disposing of corpses was to hang them from high branches in trees and leave them to the birds. Not that there's anything wrong with leaving a body up there flapping in the breeze . . .

> **I AM READY TO MEET MY MAKER, BUT WHETHER MY MAKER IS PREPARED FOR THE GREAT ORDEAL OF MEETING ME IS ANOTHER MATTER.**
>
> WINSTON CHURCHILL, PRIME MINISTER (DIED 1965)

# TOWER OF SILENCE

While very few cultures thought dead bodies were really great things, the Zoroastrians, an ancient Iranian religious sect that is still around today, felt more strongly about them than others. According to their religion, a corpse was about as close to evil as you could get and death was a loss on the great spiritual battlefield. Since there was a very real possibility that the corpse could add to the suffering of the world, it needed to be disposed of quickly, efficiently, and completely, with as little contact with anything else as possible. (Sounds like the Zoroastrians would also have had some very strong opinions on zombies.) Even fire could be polluted by the "corpse demon," so cremation was out. With limited options, the Zoroastrians decided that body exposure was the best way to protect the world from the dead.

***Since there was a very real possibility that the corpse could add to the suffering of the world, it needed to be disposed of quickly, efficiently, and completely, with as little contact with anything else as possible.***

Unlike other cultures and religions that practice body exposure as a way to dispose of their dead, the Zoroastrians took their practices a step further by building giant structures to facilitate the decay, starting in the 1500s. These dakhmas (or Towers of Silence, which would make a really awesome band name) are large round structures, usually on top of hills, where dead bodies are left for the birds. Since birds of prey need to eat anyway, the corpse is doing the little good it can for the world.

The towers were usually a few stories tall and their width seems to have depended on the size of the local population at the time they were built. More people meant more bodies, which meant more floor space was needed on the top of the tower. Corpses were placed on the "roof" with walls along the edge thankfully blocking the view of rotting bodies from passersby. While Zoroastrianism is all about gender equality, in death men and women are split up. On top of the towers are different areas for different bodies, radiating out around a hole in the center. The children are placed in the innermost ring, followed by the bodies of women, and then men.

Reports from astonished observers say that sometimes it took the birds just an hour to completely remove all the flesh from the bones. At this point someone would go back up on the tower, using the little footpaths left between the dead, and cover the skeleton in lime. After some months left bleaching in the sun, the bones were thrown down the hole where they would eventually disintegrate.

Zoroastrians still use their Towers of Silence today, especially in India. However, some areas have as few as a dozen vultures around to dispose of the bodies due to a mysterious disease killing them off, which means that the death rituals surrounding the towers are less effective and less hygienic than ever before. Skyscrapers and homes surround some of the towers, and as bodies that used to be stripped to bone within hours were now in identifiable states months after they were placed on the towers, the smell became unbearable. The editor of a large newspaper, Bombay Samachar, said he would not have wanted his dog disposed of in such a way, let alone a family member. When the problem first arose in the 1990s, Zoroastrians were divided about what should be done. Some said it was time to abandon the towers altogether, some wanted to let things take their course (no matter how smelly and unhygienic they might be), but a small minority looked to technology to save their funeral tradition.

In 2003, solar panels were installed in some towers and there was an almost immediate uproar. While the only thing being added to the death ritual was more concentrated sun, this was enough of a change that the more orthodox Zoroastrians threw a fit. But most members of the faith embraced the solar technology as the only acceptable way to speed up the decomposition process. Still, one member of the faith called the tower's new additions "glorified toasters." Regardless, the panels work, increasing the temperature on the towers to about 250 degrees, enough to dehydrate the bodies quickly, but not burn them.

Even those Zoroastrians willing to experiment with new ways of body disposal hope they don't have to rely on this technology forever. Starting in 2001, some areas with low vulture populations started their own aviaries, hoping to breed enough of the scavengers in captivity to eventually replace the ones lost to the mysterious disease. Considering they had been eating dead humans for a thousand years you really have to wonder what finally killed them off . . .

# DEATH IS FOR THE BIRDS

Tibet has its share of problems, and how to dispose of the dead has always been one of them. The earth is almost always too hard, rocky, or frozen to dig graves in any sort or realistic time frame. The barren hills are also short on fuel for fires, and the fires that they do have are put to better use keeping people alive than cremating the dead. So the region came up with something completely different . . .

These commoner funerals—if you were rich or important, people would take the time to bury you—are optimistically called sky burials, and, while possibly dating back thousands of years, the practice was first recorded in the 1200s. Buddhism is the major religion of Tibet, and since they believe the body is just a vessel for a soul until it dies and is reborn, there is nothing sacred about a corpse. Leaving a dead body out for the birds is the simplest option.

This is not to say that there are not funeral rites associated with sky burials. And done officially they are not even that cheap. The Tibetans have special locations for the exposure of the bodies throughout the country, and traveling there can be difficult. Once the location is set, the naked corpse is laid out on a large flat rock and monks will chant around it while incense burns. Then a specially trained monk will dismember the body in a special way (think butchering). Considering the personal nature of cutting a dead body up, the only people who attend sky burial funerals are usually close family, and even they often stand far enough away so they can't actually see what is happening.

Once the body is prepared, the vultures come. Most scavengers know these areas and wait in anticipation for the next funeral, sometimes the hungry birds even have to be beaten away while the ceremony is taking place. But once it is done, everyone wants the birds to dig in. Having a bunch of vultures uninterested in the corpse that was just prepared for them is considered a very bad omen. It is also important that they get every bit of flesh from the bones before they decide they are full, or bad luck will fall on the family of the deceased.

If you are too poor to afford an "official" sky burial, it is acceptable to leave a body out just about anywhere on a rock for the birds. The Chinese were pretty creeped out by this practice when they first took over Tibet in the 1950s and outlawed sky burials completely, but of course people still participated in them. Since the 1980s the government has allowed these funerals to resume, presumably since they ran up against the same problems the Tibetans had solved with vultures centuries ago.

**WE ALL PAY FOR LIFE WITH DEATH, SO EVERYTHING IN BETWEEN SHOULD BE FREE.**

BILL HICKS, COMEDIAN (DIED 1994)

## YOU'RE STANDING ON GRANDMA

These days when a relative dies your first instinct is probably not to renovate your home, but for the ancient Maya home improvements and mourning were inextricably linked. Since Mayan building materials in A.D. 500 were not able to stand up to the elements too well, Mayan homes needed to be completely rebuilt every twenty to thirty years. The roof might be leaking or the walls might be moldy, and nothing about the house was worth saving by that point. But the family would wait until someone died to start tearing things apart because the burial would be a key part of the new home.

When a relative finally kicked the bucket, the floor of the home was ripped up and the individual was buried underneath it, sometimes along with any important objects the family owned. Then the entire house and everything left inside it was set alight—something society frowns on today, even if you still can't find the perfect paint color for the living room walls after ten trips to Home Depot. Once the former home was reduced to a pile of ash, the family constructed a new home over the burial site. If another family member died a couple weeks later, too bad; they missed their chance and would be buried elsewhere.

Eventually the foundations of houses could house half a dozen bodies and various artifacts. Now archaeologists excavating the sites can see the entire history of a family through these underhome mini graveyards. Unfortunately all the unearthed artifacts are broken, indicating that not only did a person have to die to join the underground family history museum, but even inanimate objects had to "die" as well.

While the Maya are long gone, the Ifugao tribe in the Philippines (which is mostly Christianized now) still practices underhome burial to this day. After someone dies and funeral rites are celebrated they are buried in a place away from the family home for a couple years. The tribe believes that the spirit of a person resides where their bones are, so perhaps they think everyone deserves some time away from their relatives after they die (or vice versa). After this gap year from the family, the bones are exhumed and reburied under the house, in essence returning the deceased to their people. While they can be buried anywhere under their home, the kitchen is an especially popular area. Nothing beats cooking with spirits!

# THE NEVER-ENDING FUNERAL

Plenty of cultures throughout history have thrown funerals with a party atmosphere, but rarely has the deceased been as front and center as in the Buguias funerals in the Philippines. When people die they aren't shut away in a box but for a week or more are the guest of honor at a huge barbeque. Fortunately, unlike the practice of some other tribes, the deceased is not the main meal.

When a member of the tribe dies he or she is immediately put in a chair just outside the home. Since corpses aren't that great at sitting up straight, the body is tied down by the head, arms, and feet. Then begins a ceremony that can last anywhere from a few days to a few months. Without any kind of embalming, time does start to play havoc on the decomposing corpse. In a vain attempt to keep it looking nice, someone is employed to sit next to the body and swat away flies, something we can only assume is futile after a while. We can only hope that this unlucky fly swatter gets first dibs at the barbeque as compensation.

Friends and relatives start showing up with gifts of livestock, always in male and female pairs. On the first day, only enough animals to feed the mourners are slaughtered and prepared. By the third day, however, a veritable slaughterhouse is set up, with all of the guests' animals killed, as well as many animals that belonged to the deceased. The richer the person was, the more livestock gets eaten—why not, that's what they would have wanted, right? The amount of meat available indicates the deceased's status in society; for the very rich this means killing and preparing animals for months, sometimes wiping out up to half of their herds. Since more food means more people are needed to eat it, these funerals turned into almost festivals. Add lots of alcohol to the mix and you end up with people staying up all night for days at a time, eating, drinking, and sometimes breaking out into song to entertain the corpse.

***Add lots of alcohol to the mix and you end up with people staying up all night for days at a time, eating, drinking, and sometimes breaking out into song to entertain the corpse.***

After enough meat has been consumed, the deceased is finally buried. But just because they are buried in one place doesn't mean they'll be there forever. Corpses could get bored, and if they want to see another small patch of ground somewhere else, the person's spirit appears to a relative in a dream and requests a new gravesite. Of course a new burial means a whole new party, complete with almost as much meat and celebration as the first one. You could almost suspect the Buguias would literally find any excuse to party.

# THE PREDEATH PARTY

You might sometimes wonder just what people will say about you at your funeral. Some people have gone to great lengths to find out, but others take the easier way and have a funeral of sorts before their (last) big day. The most famous living funeral was that of Morrie Schwartz, the real-life protagonist of *Tuesdays with Morrie*, a book short enough that thousands of people actually read it and then sobbed over the beauty of celebrating a person's life before he or she died. Of course, living funerals have a variety of benefits over "dead" funerals, namely because you can kiss and hug the guest of honor and no one will call the police. Living funerals have become especially popular in Taiwan, which is a huge swing from just a couple generations ago, when even saying a word that sort of sounded like the word death was considered bad luck. Now people turn out in droves to attend the living funerals of the terminally ill. One twenty-five-year-old man even invited the doctors and medical students who would be getting his body after he died to his living funeral, which must have made for some awkward conversations.

One problem with living funerals is the tricky issue of timing. Ideally one would be held when the guest of honor was still well enough to enjoy it, but with some it's hard to know how accurate the doctor's estimates are about how long someone has. An eighty-five-year-old cardinal threw himself one in 2007 and two years later was still going strong. Still, no one was probably complaining, considering the alternative.

You could probably get out of attending a real funeral if money, time, or distance made it difficult, but it would be pretty difficult to turn down an invitation to a living funeral. Especially since many people who hold living funerals then eschew plans for a more traditional one after death. Considering the extra effort and emotional output necessary to pull off a living funeral, it is unofficially frowned upon to hold one unless you are actually terminally ill with a certain amount of time left to live. So, if you're not terminally ill and you thought throwing your own funeral just to hear some nice things said about you would be a great plan, then you are out of luck. People might show up, but they would all know you were totally uncouth. The point is closure, not another yearly excuse for a party—unless that's what you're looking for.

**Always go to other people's funerals, otherwise they won't come to yours.**

Yogi Berra, baseball player

# KING ME

In March 2012, King George Tupou V the absolute monarch of the tiny South Pacific country of Tonga, died at the age of sixty-three. In a lavish funeral ceremony 1,500 men all dressed in black shirts and traditional grass skirts carried the late king's body. A marching band preceded the body and thousands of people, including 5,000 schoolchildren, lined the streets to catch a glimpse of the funeral procession. And why not? The country was about to enter 100 days of mourning . . . again. The king had only been on the throne for four years, and while mourning a royal twice in less than half a decade might have been inconvenient for many people, for the forty official undertakers of the royal family it meant another three months of the cushiest job in the country.

You see, Tongan kings cannot be touched—although there must be some exception to this rule or where would the little Tongan princes come from?—and this does not stop once the king is dead; his corpse deserves just as much respect as his body did when he was alive. Enter the royal undertakers. Called the Nima Tapu, these men are allowed to prepare the body—with a huge caveat. Since their hands touched the royal body, to ensure that respect is maintained for every royal skin cell that might have come off they cannot use their hands for anything—anything—for the next 100 days. While it might sound nice to have people prepare your food and help dress you for three months, the reality of not being able to use your perfectly good hands would most likely make you go slightly crazy, especially when it came to more personal matters like going to the bathroom.

***Traditionally after an undertaker performed his duties his hands were cut off, if he was lucky. If he was unlucky he was strangled.***

Still, no matter how difficult being waited on hand and foot for months might be these days, it is a huge step up from the historical end of a royal undertaker. Nima Tapu were always people of foreign decent, usually Maori or Samoans. While this made it less of an offense for them to touch the dead king's body, it also made them more expendable. Traditionally after an undertaker performed his duties his hands were cut off, if he was lucky. If he was unlucky he was strangled. The hand mutilation wasn't limited to people who had touched the body; loved ones of the deceased, even if they were royalty themselves, would often cut off part or all of one of their fingers as a show of grief. Makes sense why today's Nima Tapu are no doubt thrilled they only have to pretend to not have any hands for a few months instead of actually not having any hands for the rest of their lives. And it sure makes those Nima Tapus handy to have around.

# THE SEARCH FOR SKELETONS

Humans have an almost pathological need to properly mourn the dead. And in most Western cultures "properly" includes burying the body in a place of the deceased's choice. Unfortunately people die in situations all the time that make it difficult, if not suicidal, to recover the bodies. That hasn't stopped anyone from trying though.

In 1962, a Navy plane crashed in Greenland and all those onboard perished. At the time, while the crash was treated as a tragedy, no one recommended risking more personnel's lives to recover the bodies. But in 1995 the story, including the fact that the bodies had just been left there for thirty years, was picked up by the media and there was a national outcry. The Navy estimated it would cost \$2–\$4 million to recover the bodies, but finally in 2004 they managed it, if only to try and save some face.

Slightly more difficult was the recovery of three crewmen who crashed in Antarctica in 1946. The Greenland recovery drew attention to the Antarctic crewmen's situation, the difference being that, at this point, they had been buried under 150 feet of snow and ice. And while both Antarctica and Greenland are very cold, Greenland is like a Hawaiian vacation compared to the conditions at the bottom of the world. After assessing all of the problems and the cost involved (estimated \$32 million) the Navy decided the bodies were not worth retrieving, a decision that angered many veterans.

Of course, the armed forces only have so much money to spend, and there are a lot more bodies out there, including an estimated 80,000 unrecovered bodies still missing from World War II alone. The good news is that the Joint POW-MIA Accounting Command (JPAC), based in Hawaii, is out there looking for those missing in action. Known as "the most honorable mission in the military," JPAC will not rest until they find the remains of every fallen serviceperson out there. This mission statement means they head to some of the most inhospitable places in the world, not just the freezing cold of Greenland, but the thickest jungles of Vietnam, even deep in the ocean. They keep finding what they are looking for, and, once they find all or part of a body, they work on narrowing it down to who it belongs to using military records and, if possible, DNA tests.

It is not just the armed forces that go to any length to recover bodies for proper burial. Years after the crash of an Air France Airbus off the coast of Brazil, divers are still working to recover bodies. While some families feel that the ocean is the best final resting place for their loved ones, others say they can't move on until their friends and relatives "come home."

## MAKING A SPLASH IN THE AFTERLIFE

Everyone thinks they know what a Viking funeral looked like: A bunch of bearded, Nordic men wearing helmets with horns on them, sends a boat laden with their chief out into the water. Once it is far enough from the shore someone shoots a flaming arrow and the boat and the body incinerate in a fitting and beautiful end for someone who spent their life at sea . . . The problem is that, according to historians, this never happened. Ever.

Vikings *were* buried in "boats," that is, boat-shaped rock formations on land. Northern Europe is covered in Viking burial mounds, most of which contain these boat graves. One of the reasons that "traditional" burial at sea could not have happened is that wood would never burn hot enough to completely destroy a body. In fact, the chances would be a lot better that a half-charred and bloated corpse would wash up on the edge of the nearest village in a couple days.

However, other cultures *do* bury their dead at sea, and in ways that are much more effective. While many religions have specific rules against sea burial, most also have exceptions for people who die at sea. In the old days when sea voyages took months and any bodies would have to be either stored on board or thrown into the sea, most cultures took the less smelly option (although not all of them. Admiral Nelson, the famous British naval hero who was killed during the Battle of Trafalgar in 1805, was famously stored in a barrel of wine on board his ship after he was shot, and popular rumor had it that the men sipped from the barrel as an act of very disgusting respect for their commander).

Most navies allow for burial at sea for current or ex-service members. Astronaut Neil Armstrong, an ex-navy man himself, was "buried" in the Atlantic Ocean after his death in 2012. However, if the individual who wishes to be buried at sea dies while on land, or at least on a ship that has a way of getting the body back to the mainland, the bodies are usually sent back for either cremation or to acquire a coffin. Coffins are key, since they solve the whole "floating corpse" problem. During wartime, if coffins cannot be easily acquired, bodies are wrapped in a heavy cloth and have weights tied to them.

While burial at sea can be one of the most dignified ways of laying someone to rest, people who don't come from boating backgrounds still find it a bit concerning. In 1979, a general strike took place in the UK. When people asked what would happen to recently deceased bodies, since the gravediggers union was part of the strike, Liverpool's medical officer of health said that if it became unhygienic, they would just bury the bodies at sea. Public uproar at his comments is cited by some pundits as helping prompt an end to the strike. Ironic, seeing as fans of Liverpool's soccer team sing a song about crossing a river.

**NO ONE ON HIS DEATHBED EVER SAID, "I WISH I HAD SPENT MORE TIME ON MY BUSINESS."**

PAUL E. TSONGAS, U.S. SENATOR (DIED 1997)

# THE LEAST YOU CAN DO

Sometimes you need a few extra people at a funeral to look sad and cry over the deceased. Maybe he didn't have many friends. Maybe you can't make it yourself and want to send someone in your place. Maybe hundreds of people showed up just to make sure that the bastard was dead and a few very loud criers would help to cover the giddy laughter and shouts of joy. Whatever the reason, the professional mourner is an ancient tradition, and one that is now becoming a legitimate option for out-of-work actors in some parts of the world.

At one point in history, professional mourning, where people with no connection to the deceased were paid to show up at the funeral and cry loudly, was popular enough that it is actually mentioned in the Bible ("And lo, Jesus brought Lazarus back from the dead and upon waking he said, 'Wait, is this really everybody? Could you guys not have at least paid some people to pretend to miss me?'"). In China it dates back to around 156 B.C. Mourners were paid large sums to cry and shriek loudly, pull their hair, and even crawl on the ground, just like young girls attending a Justin Bieber concert today. The idea was both to make the deceased look more missed and to set a tone that allowed other mourners to cry and wail and not look weird.

An 1877 article in the *New York Times* noted the popularity of these "Oriental hired mourners." The journalist wondered why such an obvious business proposition hadn't made it to America yet, the land where you can pay anyone to do literally anything and call it freedom. Of course, it being the Industrial Age, he felt the United States would have to improve on the idea by making a steam-powered mechanical mourner, "A four-horsepower mourner would doubtless produce more heart-rending shrieks in the course of half an hour than [a normal man] could utter in a day." He had obviously never listened to Bjork.

Meanwhile, in England, the Victorians would never be caught dead expressing so much emotion at a funeral (keep calm and carry the coffin), but they had their own take on professional mourners. Illustrating perfectly how one was expected to behave at the time, these men were called "Mutes." They were usually lower class men who were given a nice suit and some money to show up at a funeral, say nothing, and look very, very sad. Considering they were usually poor or working-class men being paid a pittance to show up at some rich guy's funeral that cost more than what they would earn in a lifetime, this was probably pretty easy to achieve. The practice started in the 1700s, but by the mid-1800s no decent person would be caught dead without a mute or two. Then Charles Dickens poked fun at the practice in *Oliver Twist*, and what Dickens hated, everyone hated. Satirical magazines of the time also started to point out that these seemingly dour and respectable men usually took their money and got drunk right after the service. By the turn of the century, mutes had been laughed out of a job in England, probably cheered up by the proper application of irony.

Professional mourners also had a brief popularity in Italy after World War II, but these days the practice continues mainly in the Ivory Coast and China. In the African country whole families can make a good living out of mourning at funerals, which there are a whole lot of. Would-be mourners hang around outside funeral homes, read the obituaries in newspapers, and contact wealthy families asking if they need a few extra people to sob over the coffin. The best performers become famous in their field and bereaved families contact them directly, asking for their services. According to one professional, being a good actor is key: If you can't cry on demand, you have to up the ante on the hair pulling and wailing, "Even if you are paid for this job, you have to have the passion for it."

***At least one company exists that offers thirty to forty-five minutes of sobbing by a grave for just $500. Thanks to their services you can please your ancestors and still make that business meeting.***

The Cultural Revolution put a stop to the practice in China, but recently paying people to mourn for you has come back into fashion there in a big way. The Qingming Festival is a day when the Chinese honor their ancestors and visit their gravesites, but with people's lives getting more and more hectic, some people find themselves too busy to visit the graves themselves. At least one company exists that offers thirty to forty-five minutes of sobbing by a grave for just $500. Thanks to their services you can please your ancestors and still make that business meeting.

# STRIPPER FUNERALS

Funerals are usually pretty depressing events, but some cultures have come up with ways to make them a bit more exciting; of note is the Irish addition of alcohol to the wake, but no one is as creative as the Taiwanese. And that's because, at many funerals on the island, strippers entertain both the living and the dead.

While getting naked at funerals was outlawed by an embarrassed Taiwanese government in the 1980s, this hasn't stopped its popularity in more rural areas. The traveling performers arrive on the back of large tricked-out trucks known as Electric Flower Cars, and start doing their thing. Even if the family requests that none of the performers actually get completely naked, most sing and pole dance while stripping down to bikinis. Lap dances are also not unheard of, although hopefully only for the living. The more noise and excitement the strippers contribute, the better, since Taiwanese funerals are not expected to be quiet, somber occasions.

Funeral stripteases may have been born when the country's mafia got into the mortuary business. Since the mafia already controlled many strip clubs, combining the two meant more money for organized crime. They convinced people to go along with the bizarre idea by pointing out that the entertainment would attract more mourners to the event, and since the number of people attending a funeral was a big deal in Taiwanese society, it caught on. Some people even insist that there is a supernatural reasoning behind the shows, saying that older ghosts are jealous of newer ghosts and likely to pick on your late relative, but the sight of naked ladies will distract them and ensure that the deceased enters the afterlife in peace. Certainly brings a new meaning to raising the dead.

These days the idea has spread to parts of mainland China as well. In some areas, a funeral might be the best entertainment available that night. It's almost certainly better than going to a karaoke bar. In fact, it is not unheard of for two funerals to happen at once, with the performers competing to see who can draw the most mourners to their ceremony. However, it's important to note that the Chinese government is just as unhappy with their stripper funerals as the Taiwanese government was, and has set up a hotline where people can report "funeral misdeeds." At least five people have been arrested in the past few years for promoting these "obscene" sendoffs. But the determined ones will not be deterred by the threat of jail time. One Taiwanese man who loved strip clubs and would travel all over to attend new ones made a bet with his son that if he lived to be 100 he could have a stripper at his funeral. He made it to 103, and true to his word, his son hired his father's favorite entertainment to send him off in style.

**LIFE IS HARD. THEN YOU DIE. THEN THEY THROW DIRT IN YOUR FACE. THEN THE WORMS EAT YOU. BE GRATEFUL IT HAPPENS IN THAT ORDER.**

DAVID GERROLD, WRITER

# DEAD DANCE PARTY

For the Malagasy people of Madagascar, dying doesn't mean you can stop turning up at family reunions. That's because every few years the tomb where your dead relatives are housed is opened, and it's party time!

Some of the Malagasy tribes believe that the soul of a person doesn't leave the physical world until their body has completely decomposed. Clearly, being trapped in a crypt for years on end can get really boring—especially if you weren't really close to some of the other family members now sharing your tomb. So, starting on the first anniversary of a loved one's death, and about every seventh anniversary thereafter, the whole family gets together and pulls the still-intact bodies of their ancestors out of storage in a ceremony called Famadihana, or "turning of the bones." A more accurate description would be "dancing around with dead bodies." While any number of corpses can take part in the ritual, the most important one is always someone who has not been part of the celebrations before. The gatherings may have been influenced by Southeast Asian funeral customs and seem to date from the 1600s. The get-togethers can be enormous, with relatives traveling from across the country and even abroad to attend, because really, how often do you get to do the foxtrot with a corpse?

***While a band plays live music, the relatives hold the bodies above their heads and dance around with them. This can go on for hours while hundreds of relatives, friends, or even random tourists get drunk and buy cigarettes from makeshift stalls set up just for the celebration.***

While a band plays live music, the relatives hold the bodies above their heads and dance around with them. This can go on for hours while hundreds of relatives, friends, or even random tourists get drunk and buy cigarettes from makeshift stalls set up just for the celebration. After the dancing is over, the silk shrouds wrapped around the most solid corpses are changed, while those who have fallen to bits (possibly helped along by the whole dancing thing) are adjusted back into a vaguely human shape. Relatives run their hands over the deceased, relaying family news and gossip, and asking for blessings like good health and wealth. Various family members and any invited local officials give speeches, and then everyone pretty much continues to get drunk. At the end of the celebrations, which can go on for two or three days, the newly shrouded bodies are relabeled and placed back in the crypt with presents from the living. Not surprisingly, considering how booze-soaked the celebrations are, one popular gift is alcohol. The tomb is resealed and everyone returns home to nurse their hangover until the next Famadihana. Some Protestant churches have tried to put a stop to Famadihanas, but the Catholic Church allows them because it sees them as cultural, rather than religious, celebrations. However, these events are not cheap, as the people holding them pay for the musicians, new shrouds, a feast for hundreds of revelers, and the crazy amount of alcohol needed to convince people that dancing around with corpses is a good idea. But even in Madagascar, one of the poorest countries in the world, the cost is seen as worth it thanks to the importance of these family reunions.

# FANTASY COFFINS

In 1989, visitors to the National Museum of Modern Art gazed upon something a bit more fanciful than the expected all-white painting or upside-down urinal. For the first time, Westerners were introduced to the superb craftsmanship of Kane Kwei, a specialty coffin maker in Ghana.

Kwei wasn't originally in the coffin trade. He built decorative chairs for local dignitaries to sit on during processions. His career change came about by chance in the 1950s when one of those dignitaries requested that his chair actually be shaped like a cocoa bean. When the man died right before the parade the people in charge decided to bury him in the perfectly shaped "chair" instead. Shortly afterward Kwei's grandmother died. Since she had always wanted to travel but had never got around to it, he designed an airplane coffin so she could "travel after death." By this point people started hearing about Kwei's creative coffin making, and his third customer was a fisherman who wanted to be buried in a canoe. After that, the popularity of his fantasy coffins grew rapidly. There were so many requests for coffins that reflected the personality of the deceased in a literal sense that Kwei took on apprentices, many of whom eventually left to start their own figurative coffin businesses. These days, in parts of Ghana, you're actually much less likely to see a traditional box coffin than one shaped like a chicken or a cell phone.

And despite the fanciful coffins that can look like anything—including fish, battleships, angels, Cadillacs, hammers, elephants, lions, Coke bottles, and shoes (just to name a few)—the burials are taken very seriously indeed. The local religion, a combination of Christianity and folk traditions, says that the coffins will please the deceased and carry them into the afterlife, and that making your ancestors happy right from the beginning is a good thing for your future happiness. Future happiness aside, the craftsmanship on the coffins is exquisite, making them worthy of display in museums, but the art of the craftsman is somewhat wasted on the actual coffins. The family only sees the coffin for the first time on the day of the burial and then it goes straight into the ground.

After Kwei's exhibition in Paris, other coffin makers were invited to show around the world, but it was not until pictures of these crazy coffins started showing up on the Internet that the rest of the world really took note. Now the craftsmen report regular commissions from all around the world. And while the city of Accra is not the first place you might think of as a must-see destination, thanks to people's fascination with the coffins the city is seeing a boom in foreign visitors. It seems tourists are just dying to visit.

**My wallpaper and I are fighting a duel to the death. One of us has got to go.**

Oscar Wilde, writer (died 1900)

# POSTMORTEM MARRIAGES

While marrying a dead person might not seem like the most obvious idea in the world, four different cultures on three continents came up with it independently, so there must be something to the concept. And while not as common as in the big four (France, China, India, and the Sudan) posthumous marriage ceremonies have taken place in dozens of other countries around the world. So if your mother has been nagging you about how far above the average marriage age you are and why can't you settle down already, just reassure her that you literally have all eternity.

In France, these marriages tend to be performed if a woman's fiancé dies prior to her wedding ceremony. The practice seems to have originated during World War I when women wanted to honor their relationships with soldiers who had died at the front. Considering the few eligible young men left after the war, a ghost marriage was probably one of your better options. After a dam collapsed in the 1950s, one woman asked the president of France for permission to marry her fiancé, who had drowned. A lot of media attention followed, and a law was quickly drafted making posthumous marriage legal in France. But not just anyone can qualify; you must petition the president himself, prove you were engaged, and get approval from the deceased's family, so modern-day Romeos and Juliets need not apply. Even with all these hoops to jump through, 75 percent of the hundreds of applications submitted every year are successful. Once the application is approved, an actual marriage ceremony is performed, with a photo usually standing in for the corpse (since decomposition is generally considered a real turn off). The wedding also legally legitimizes any children the couple had out of wedlock. Instead of a wife, the woman (and it is usually a woman) legally becomes a widow. However, the marriage does not allow her to collect any inheritance the deceased might have had coming, so the bride doesn't have to go straight from the altar to a lawyer's office to fight over the will.

In China, ghost marriages used to be much more common than they are today. It was important that a woman get married because she would join her husband's family and have children, and her descendants would worship her as part of that family. This put a lot more pressure on spinsters than the more average prospect of simply owning a dozen cats. If a woman died before she got hitched, she might be married off to an unwed dead man. This would unite the families and allow his relatives to pray for her. If a living woman remained unmarried, she could marry a dead man for the same reason. Marrying off a deceased son to a live woman had benefits for the son's family as well. Even though the woman was expected to be loyal to her husband, and therefore celibate her whole life (unless she was into some really icky sexual stuff), the presence of a "wife" in the family would allow the husband's parents to adopt a child in his name. This child would then be considered his legitimate heir. Without a wife, adopting was impossible.

Despite the Communist Party's attempt to put an end to ghost marriages in 1949, they still occur today. In 2012, grave robbers were arrested for stealing a recently deceased woman's corpse and trying to sell her in marriage, and, in 2007, a man admitted to killing at least six women and selling them as brides. These bodies, and the celestial marriages they represent, reportedly sell for thousands of dollars, making dead adult women worth more in parts of Chinese society than living baby girls.

# SAYING GOODBYE TO FIDO

If you've ever owned a pet, you know that the loss of one can hurt just as bad as the loss of a friend or relative. As far as we can tell, there has never been a point in human history where it has not been this way. Graves indicating ritualized burial for animals have been discovered dating to at least 2500 B.C., and both Alexander the Great and the Egyptian pharaohs built great tombs for their most beloved dogs and horses. The regular people of the ancient world set aside huge areas specifically for burying their pets. And to think you flushed your goldfish down the toilet. You should be ashamed!

Openly displaying devotion to pets seems to have died out a bit in Europe during the Middle Ages, possibly due to accusations of witchcraft for women in particular who seemed too close to their animals. But by the Victorian era, when obsession with death reached new heights, pet funerals came back in a big way. This was easy enough for people in the country, but in the crowded cities dead animals were carted away with the trash or thrown into a river; 3,000 deceased pets were pulled from the Seine in 1899 alone. City dwellers, desperate to find a more acceptable final resting place for their beloved pets, started sneaking into human cemeteries to bury their animals in the dead of night. The animals were placed in little coffins, often on a pillow, and buried with a bone or favorite toy, a tradition that carries on to this day.

These days pet burial is big business. The International Association of Pet Cemeteries and Crematories enforces regulations and counts thousands of members, more than 500 of which are in the United States alone. You can buy everything from gold coffins to $1000 burial plots for your beloved pet. But these days, the new trend is taking that devotion a step further and you can actually be buried with your pet.

Most human cemeteries specifically do not allow animal burials. Therefore the choices for someone who wants to spend eternity next to their best friend are limited. One way of getting around this is cremation. Human ashes are allowed to be buried or scattered almost anywhere, so people started leaving requests to be cremated and then buried next to their dog or cat in a pet cemetery. In 2011, a pet cemetery in New York where at least 700 humans had chosen to be laid to rest with their pets in the last century suddenly banned the practice. Almost immediately they found themselves on the wrong end of a firestorm of controversy and quickly backed down. Let this be a lesson to anyone else who might try something similar: you do not mess with a person who just lost a pet. Today, brand-new burial sites are opening with the express purpose of letting humans and animals be together for eternity. And in 2010 the first joint human/animal cemetery opened in England, indicating that this trend may soon be a global one. What fun! You will have all eternity to teach your dog new tricks—like how to roll over in the grave and play alive.

**THE GREAT THING ABOUT THE DEAD, THEY MAKE SPACE.**

JOHN UPDIKE, AUTHOR (DIED 2009)

# NOT-SO-SOLEMN SUPERLATIVES

No matter how much time you spend planning your funeral, there will be someone out there who did it better, fancier, faster, or just plain cooler. Not content with simply outdoing each other during their lifetimes, people have been pushing death to the limit as well. Whether it is the ongoing argument over just which is the largest cemetery in the world, or who managed to get the largest turnout when they died, funeral records are important. And when it comes to those that are tracked by the *Guinness Book of World Records*, they are challenged and broken all the time. Maybe you want to be one of the millions to take a macabre trip to the most visited cemetery in the world, or get tips on how to hold a classy funeral for your dog. Even if you just want to live the good life in death and go out with the most expensive hearse, casket, and burial plot, the superlatives in this chapter are made just for you.

## THE MOST POPULAR CEMETERY NAME

While the settlers of the Wild West were undoubtedly good at enduring hardship, building something from nothing, and annihilating populations (both Native American and buffalo), they were not so good on the creative front. Towns were named for towns that already existed or for a natural landmark. And those were the important names! When it came to naming cemeteries virtually everybody went with the same one: Boot Hill.

Dodge City, Kansas, was the first to come up with the moniker. Since this was the Old West, a large number of men seemed to die "with their boots on." Not while laid up in bed from some illness but usually in the middle of the street or a saloon from a bullet wound, or what was fancifully referred to as "lead poisoning." Since many of the men would not have wanted their families to know how they died, a statistically unlikely number of tombstones claimed the owner had been struck by lightning.

The popularity of the name was astonishing, and soon hundreds of towns had a Boot Hill, but the most famous ones include those in Deadwood, South Dakota, and Tombstone, Arizona. Tombstone's Boothill, which although no one has been buried there in more than 100 years is still open to the public today, is most famous as the burial site of Billy Clanton, Frank McLaury, and Tom McLaury, the three men killed by Doc Holliday and the Earp brothers at the O.K. Corral. Boot Hill, South Dakota, now called Mount Moriah, is most famous as the final resting place for the cowboy Wild Bill Hickok as well as his friend Calamity Jane.

The greatest person to be buried in any Boot Hill has to be the late Lester Moore. While a minor historical figure, he is remembered and celebrated today for his tombstone. While working as a mail clerk for Wells Fargo he found himself in a bit of trouble. A man named Hank Dunstan came in to pick up a package and found it had been severely damaged during shipping. Hank was unimpressed, and the men settled it the Wild West way, with bullets. Dustan got off four shots but before Moore died he managed to return fire, mortally wounding his opponent. (History doesn't record what was in the mangled packages, but it better have been a dragon egg or something worth the lives of two men.) Moore was buried in Tombstone's Boothill, and the inscription on his grave made him famous:

If you are thinking of starting up your own cemetery, why not stick with what you know works and call it Boot Hill? Soon you will have modern day cowboys literally dying to be buried there.

# THE LARGEST CEMETERY

There are numerous problems with trying to declare one cemetery the largest. First of all, what type of large are we talking about: The area, the number of bodies, or a combination of both? While many cemeteries claim to be the largest, there are three good contenders on three different continents.

## OHLSDORF CEMETERY

Founded in 1877, the Ohlsdorf Cemetery in Hamburg, Germany, is the largest nonmilitary cemetery in the world when it comes to area. While it may not have the largest number of bodies, it is still home to an impressive 1.5 million dead people. The 966-acre space is a popular tourist attraction and is so large that it requires twenty-five bus stops for people to get from place to place without exhausting themselves. It also takes 230 gardeners just to keep the cemetery looking nice.

This being Germany (where they are a bit touchy about the whole World War II thing), there are six memorials for victims of the Nazis, and those buried there include such dignitaries as a former German chancellor, a Nobel Prize winner, and numerous Hamburg mayors. The most controversial burial may have been in 2011, when a young porn star named Carolin Wosnitza was buried in the cemetery. Her profession was not a problem, since one of Germany's most famous prostitutes, Domenica Niehoff, is also buried there, but Carolin's $25,000 tombstone and memorial, which included pictures of her in lingerie, was deemed "too sexy," and the cemetery boss demanded its removal.

## CALVERTON NATIONAL CEMETERY

The largest military cemetery in the world in terms of size is Calverton National Cemetery. Located on Long Island, it is new to the grave game, only opening in 1978. Even though it spreads over

1,000 acres, Calverton is filling up fast, with more than 200,000 interments already and another 7,000 per year at present. Funerals there occur so often that the cemetery has set up almost an assembly-line process of burying people, allowing numerous interments to occur at once.

### WADI-US-SALAAM

When it comes to number of bodies, nobody beats Wadi-us-Salaam, or the Valley of Peace, in Iraq. An estimated 5 million people have been buried there since its founding in the 600s. According to some reports, virtually every Shia Muslim in Iraq requests to be buried there. Tombs in the cemetery include numerous prophets and Imams, including the first Shia Imam Ali ibn Abi Talib. The Valley of Peace has however been much less peaceful since the U.S. invasion of Iraq, with numerous firefights breaking out in the cemetery. Militia members use the tombs as hiding places, and one armed forces member described the act of fighting in a cemetery as "really creepy." At least there's plenty of cover . . .

**I'M ALWAYS RELIEVED WHEN SOMEONE IS DELIVERING A EULOGY AND I REALIZE I'M LISTENING TO IT.**

George Carlin, comedian (died 2008)

## THE FUNNIEST CEMETERY

While some cultures see death as a moderately happy occasion, European tradition is pretty solid in the "death is serious and sad" camp. This in turn makes the Merry Cemetery in Sapanta, Romania, known as the funniest cemetery in the world, particularly disconcerting. Founded in the 1930s by Stan Ioan Patras, a local craftsman, all of the graves are topped by wooden arrow-shaped carvings that are all painted in bright and cheery colors and include informative and usually quite funny depictions and descriptions of the deceased. This fun and satirical outlook at death may have been influenced by the ancient local religion Zalmoxian and the belief that death is just a way of changing your location; it's like moving house, without having to move all your hoarded belongings, too.

The wooden tombstones in the cemetery are all hand carved. The top part includes a cartoony representation of the deceased, usually doing something related to their occupation. The bottom half includes the epitaph explaining relevant information about the dearly departed, although just how relevant in some cases can certainly be debated. The carvings are then painted in bright colors, with blue predominant throughout the cemetery. The final product is quite astonishing looking and the area is understandably a tourist attraction. Even Romanian dictator Nicolae Ceausescu visited the cemetery in 1974.

The images on the 600 or so graves sometimes imply how the deceased met their end. For example, one depicts a shepherd tending his flock, unaware of the robber who will kill him standing right behind him. Another shows a man with his beloved horses, but as we know from the epitaph, "When sitting on a mound of grass on a wagon pulled by a horse, I fell and was killed." Those hilarious Romanians, always ready with a laugh.

***Most of the descriptions are written from the deceased's point of view and sometimes include more information than you could ever want. One man hopes there are cheese sandwiches in heaven. Another man reflects on how nice and handsome he was and how so few men were like him . . .***

Most of the descriptions are written from the deceased's point of view and sometimes include more information than you could ever want. One man hopes there are cheese sandwiches in heaven. Another man reflects on how nice and handsome he was and how so few men were like him. The most famous epitaph is one not written from the dead's point of view. Instead, a woman's son-in-law came up with the verse, and we can only assume their relationship was volatile. He says if she had lived just a few more days her presence would have killed him, and that he promises to behave well from then on to make sure she can never return from hell to "bite his head off."

It's worth mentioning that Patras, the cemetery's founder, died in 1977, but not before hiring an apprentice—and carving his own grave marker, which says:

Since I was a little boy
I was known as Stan Ioan Pătraş
Listen to me, fellows
There are no lies in what I am going to say
All along my life
I meant no harm to anyone
But did good as much as I could
To anyone who asked
Oh, my poor World
Because it was hard living in it

# THE MOST EXPENSIVE PATCHES OF DIRT IN THE WORLD

Keeping up with the Joneses isn't just for the living. Even when you die there are certain graveyards that are a cut above the rest, and like anything else exclusive in life, you will pay out the nose for them. Of course, there are perks to owning some of the most coveted land in the world, none of which you will actually be able to appreciate, since you'll be dead once you start occupying it. Still, it might mean the family visits more, assuming they're not in the Maldives drinking their inheritance away.

## SANTA BARBARA CEMETERY

The Santa Barbara Cemetery would have been the perfect place for some multimillion-dollar houses. Instead, people visiting their relatives get some of the best views in the country: The graves overlook the ocean and the cemetery is filled with palm trees. Gardeners keep the grass as immaculate as at any of the many golf courses in the area. The tombs on the property are not so much tombs as Greek temples. And if you want to have a view of the Pacific for eternity it will only set you back $85,000. That's not for one of those fancy mausoleums, which go for millions, it's just for a plot closest to the cliff edge.

## FOREST LAWN MEMORIAL PARK

The most exclusive place to be buried in Hollywood is the famous Forest Lawn Memorial Park. Founded in 1906 as a not-for-profit cemetery, the owners were committed to making it the most beautiful cemetery in the world, and for a long time, this included excluding anyone who wasn't white and Christian from being buried there. Slightly less controversial was their focus on artwork; the grounds are dotted with hundreds of sculptures. Literally hundreds of famous people from the entertainment industry are buried there, and if you want to join them in a sweet mausoleum of your own, it will only set you back $825,000. Oddly enough, the three chapels on site are popular not only for funerals but weddings; Ronald Reagan married his first wife in one of them.

### WOODLAWN CEMETERY

Perhaps the most expensive graveyard in the world is Woodlawn Cemetery in the Bronx. The final resting place of New York City's great and good since 1863, Woodlawn merited a place on the U.S. National Register of Historic Places and is designated as a U.S. National Historic Landmark. While even the cheapest plots in the cemetery will run you more per square foot than you paid for your home, the kicker is the cost for enough land to build a family mausoleum. How much? A cool $1.5 million. Looks like you need to *really* love your family to set them up for all eternity at Woodlawn!

**DYING IS EASY, IT'S LIVING THAT SCARES ME TO DEATH.**

ANNIE LENNOX, SINGER-SONGWRITER

# THE MOST EXPENSIVE COFFINS

If you've managed to snag a spot in one of the most expensive cemeteries in the world, and plan on being carried to your final resting place in the most expensive hearse in the world, you better make sure that your coffin is made of more than just some cheap plywood. Fortunately there are plenty of companies ready to sell you exorbitantly priced boxes that cater to all the creature comforts that your corpse will in no way appreciate.

If you want the best of the best of something, or at least the gaudiest and most expensive, it's a good rule of thumb to copy whatever Michael Jackson did in the same situation. Even though the King of Pop died relatively young, he had already picked out his coffin. Jackson was inspired by James Brown, the Godfather of Soul's choice of casket a few years before, and it's a good thing he went big. If you watched Jackson's memorial on TV, the coffin, situated front and center, was hard to miss, considering it was completely gold plated and shined like a mirror. Called the Promethean, the casket is solid bronze, 14-carat gold plated, and has a plush blue velvet interior.

The Promethean and caskets like it go for about $30,000, although it isn't known if Jackson's was custom made with costly extras. But ridiculously over the top coffins are big business, especially in Southeast Asia. As people in the region get richer they want to go out in the style they grew accustomed to in life. Gold-plated coffins are particularly popular, but if you want something really pricey, or at least a lot less gaudy, there is another option.

Malaysian funeral director Datuk Frank Choo Chuo Siong offers his clients (or anyone willing to pay import costs) a $40,000 casket made out of solid mahogany. The outside is carved by hand with exquisite detailing, while the inside is lined with a deep red velvet. To assure the corpse the ultimate in afterlife comfort—while proving that IQ can indeed go down as wealth goes up—the headrest is adjustable. That's right, you can make sure your dead, decomposing corpse or that of your loved one doesn't get neck strain. Chuo Siong says some people are just willing to go the extra mile (or dollar) for their family members. It probably helps that they are making him rich in the process.

***Malaysian funeral director Datuk Frank Choo Chuo Siong offers his clients (or anyone willing to pay import costs) a $40,000 casket made out of solid mahogany. The outside is carved by hand with exquisite detailing, while the inside is lined with a deep red velvet.***

And, if you want to be cremated and feel left out of all this conspicuous spending, don't worry, there is a market waiting to take your cash as well. One Malaysian bereavement company offers $60,000 burial urns made of solid jade.

# THE LARGEST FUNERALS

When someone important and beloved enough dies, his or her funeral becomes a social event where people come together to express their grief, even if the sheer number of mourners mean that none of them will ever get near the coffin. And while Princess Diana, Pope John Paul II, and Michael Jackson might have had large numbers of mourners celebrating their lives from the comfort of their own homes via television, complete with pizza and beer, the number of people who actually turned out is nothing compared to some of the largest funeral gatherings of all time.

## VICTOR HUGO

While the funeral for the author Victor Hugo only drew about 2 million people, when you compare it to the population of Paris at the time it becomes one of the largest turnouts percentage-wise in history. Hugo, author of *Les Misérables,* was unbelievably popular with the French, and four years before he died a parade in his honor drew almost as many people as his funeral. When he died, the *New York Times* reported that hundreds of thousands of people were forced to sleep outside in the rain because all of the hotel rooms in Paris were booked. While the police were out in force due to rumors of unrest, the funeral was completely peaceful and went off without a hitch.

## AYATOLLAH KHOMEINI

Ayatollah Khomeini was so popular when he died in 1989 that his inner circle delayed reporting his death until they had prepared his successor. Iran could not afford a backlash against the new Ayatollah. Once news of his death leaked out people began gathering in the streets. His body was hastily displayed on top of shipping containers in the middle of nowhere to make room for the hundreds of thousands who had already turned out. At least eight people were killed in the crush to see the body. By the time his body was buried, an estimated 9 million people had taken to the streets in mourning.

### ANNA

But the *Guinness Book of World Records*–certified largest funeral gathering of all time was for Conjeevaram Natarajan Annadurai, an Indian politician known as Anna. He died in 1969 at the age of fifty-nine after cancer treatments failed. An estimated 15 million people turned out to mourn him, making it not only the most attended funeral of all time by far, but one of the top three largest peaceful gatherings in history.

# THE FASTEST HEARSES

If you ever find yourself in a situation where you need to get a dead body to a graveyard really, ridiculously quickly, don't worry. Almost every type of hearse has been tested for a speed record at some point in history, and despite their weight, those things can really fly. Obviously a standard Lincoln or Cadillac hearse is too big and heavy to go all that quickly, but that is where motorcycle hearses come in.

While motorcycle hearses exist in most countries, there seems to be quite a penchant for them in England, particularly among clergymen. Apparently after conducting dozens of funerals, men of the cloth started to figure out how they could make them go by a bit quicker. In 2011, the Reverend Ray Biddiss went for the Guinness World Record for fastest hearse in a custom bike he had spent the past four years perfecting. Although the finished product did have three wheels and a necessary boxy extension on the back to carry a coffin, the Reverend assured people it did not count as a sidecar, as he "would not be caught dead in a sidecar." Presumably he would not let his dead passenger sit in a sidecar either, since they can't help with the turns.

Biddiss named his hearse-bike the Rocket and during his official record test got it up to 114 miles an hour, with a 6-foot coffin inside. While no one was forced to lie in the coffin on a motorbike going over 100 miles an hour just for the attempt, one can assume that the weight of another body would make it a bit slower in an actual situation. That and the fact that going that fast would be illegal on actual roads . . .

Only a year later yet another English pastor decided to try to beat that record. Pastor Paul Sinclair, who goes by the nickname Faster Pastor, is a serious motorcycle nut. He says making a biker travel to his or her final resting place in a car is akin to burying a Muslim in a Christian ceremony, or a sports fan in the jersey of their rival team. To this end he set up his own hearse-bike company in 2002. In 2012, he took one of his best examples out for a record-breaking attempt. Unlike the Rocket, this bike did have the hearse contained in a sidecar as opposed to behind the bike—something sure to divide any enthusiasts who need to get to a funeral at breakneck speeds—but the reverend was successful in his attempt, hitting 117.6 miles per hour. We can only assume that somewhere deep in a cathedral more ministers are revving up for next year.

**DEATH AIN'T NOTHING BUT A FASTBALL ON THE OUTSIDE CORNER.**

AUGUST WILSON, PLAYWRIGHT

## THE MOST BEAUTIFUL TOMBSTONES

Beauty may be in the eye of the beholder, but when it comes to the beauty of death, you would be hard-pressed to find a larger collection of gorgeous tombstones than those covering the graves of hundreds of Knights of Malta in St. John's Co-Cathedral, located on the island they take their name from.

The Knights of Malta were first formed to give medical aid to Christians who made pilgrimages to the Holy Land. Once Jerusalem fell, the Knights retreated to Europe, eventually setting up their headquarters on the island of Malta in the Mediterranean. There in 1572, a cathedral was built in honor of their military victories over the Ottomans (never mind the fact that the Ottomans beat them a great deal more than they beat the Ottomans, hence why they had to leave the Holy Land in the first place). Since everyone was in a military state of mind (pretty much the standard at the time), the outside of the cathedral was more like a fort, and the inside wasn't much more interesting. But by the fancy 1600s everyone realized the gloomy interior needed something a bit fancier. Around that time important Knights of the Order started being buried in the cathedral, and their graves added to its splendor.

Over the next two centuries the floor of the church was covered wall to wall with marble slabs. Each of these represented the grave of the knight resting beneath; the more important the knight, the closer he got to be to the altar. But all of those marble slabs were about as fancy as you could get. First of all, the marble wasn't solid. It was inlaid in minute detail, with each grave usually displaying the knight's coat of arms as well as a lengthy verse about his life. Other popular themes included skulls and angels. And all were inlaid by hand out of expensive and colorful marble. If commissioned today the slabs would cost far more than even the most elaborate modern tombstone.

The overall look is stunning, if a bit schizophrenic and crowded. There is hardly an inch of the floor that is not covered in these tombstones. The epitaphs include lofty ideas about the philosophical side of death as well as the harsh realities, including the fact that one knight died of "an intestinal disease, short but intensely vile." Even back then gut rot was a mighty foe. During World War II these macabre works of art were almost lost when the cathedral was hit in a bombing raid. While everything else of value had been removed, the Knights couldn't very well dig up the entire floor.

**I HATE FUNERALS AND WOULD NOT ATTEND MY OWN IF IT COULD BE AVOIDED.**

Robert T. Morris, computer scientist

# THE MOST BITTER CEMETERY

While Arlington National Cemetery may be hallowed ground to Americans today, it started out as nothing more than a big old middle finger to the Confederacy. You see, before it was a national graveyard, Arlington was a plantation, prime land just across the Potomac from the U.S. capital. George Washington's adopted grandson passed it down to his daughter in 1857. This alone would make the location noteworthy, but that daughter, Mary Custis went on to marry General Robert E. Lee, and after the attack on Fort Sumter the estate went from interesting historical footnote to the home of the number one rebel—and that pissed a lot of important people off.

Realizing that pretty much the worst place for her was within a couple miles of the people trying to kill her husband, Mary Lee fled her home shortly after the war started. The army looked at the large house just sitting vacant and decided it was the perfect place to house a few thousand soldiers and plot the downfall of the owner. It's a given that the soldiers were very respectful of the rebel leader's things and did not pee in all the teapots.

***As the war dragged on and more and more dead soldiers arrived newly embalmed to be buried around Washington, D.C., local graveyards started to fill up, and the quartermaster general of the U.S. Army, Montgomery Cunningham Meigs, was tasked with finding new places to bury the dead.***

As the war dragged on and more and more dead soldiers arrived newly embalmed to be buried around Washington, D.C., local graveyards started to fill up, and the quartermaster general of the U.S. Army, Montgomery Cunningham Meigs, was tasked with finding new places to bury the dead. Now, Washington, D.C., was basically open swampland at this point, and there were lots of places that would have made convenient graveyards, but Meigs knew there was only one place that fit the bill, and that was the front yard of Lee's lovely home. He started burying officers there, making sure some of them even touched the house. That way, if the general came home right as the zombie apocalypse began, the late officers would have a much shorter shuffle to get to him.

As the war started to wind down, one of Lee's relatives visited the plantation and came to the conclusion it would still be livable if the bodies were removed. (This of course raises the question of just how clean the house itself was after a few years of hundreds of soldiers using the bathrooms.) But Meigs was having none of that. As far as he was concerned Lee was a traitor and if he insisted on coming home it would be to the stench of death. Determined to make the house and land completely uninhabitable for its traitor owner, he ordered that thousands more bodies be interred around the plantation.

After the war, the land reverted to the Lee family, but the government, just as pissed at Lee as Meigs was, found a sneaky way to seize it. Since Mary Lee had failed to pay the property taxes due on the land for the past few years (understandable since, you know, she was literally at war with the people who were taxing her) the plantation was taken as a tax lien. The amount owed was almost trivial, and the act was obvious to everyone for what it was: a barely legal attempt to get revenge on the Lee family. The case ended up in court, and in 1882 the Supreme Court ruled that the land was illegally confiscated and that the government had to return it to the family dead-body free. Realizing that forcing the government to move 17,000 soldiers, including some highly decorated Union officers, might not be the best PR for his family, Lee's son Custis agreed to sell the property to the nation.

Meigs was particularly happy about this result. After the war he had not given up control of the cemetery and continued to be personally involved in burying even more soldiers there, even when the Lee family technically owned the place again. Once you got the man burying bodies it was hard to stop him. Meigs also embarked on various building projects on the land to memorialize Union generals, and of course one for himself, in honor of his continued efforts to ruin one guy's house. When crowds started attending memorial celebrations at the old plantation he ordered trees cut down and an amphitheater built to house the visitors. Then, when the U.S. government officially took control of the land in 1883, Meigs ordered a "Temple of Fame" constructed to celebrate the event, right in the middle of what was once the Lee's flower garden. At least it wasn't a vineyard, otherwise there would have been sour grapes to go around.

# THE SMALLEST TOMBSTONE IN THE WORLD

In a quiet corner of the Oak Hill Cemetery in Missouri, you might stumble, literally, on the smallest tombstone in the world. Measuring about 5 by 4 by 3 inches, the marker is so small that it is attached to the ground with an iron bar to both keep it in place and allow it to be flipped over. One side contains the name of the deceased, Linnie Crouch, the other just her date of death, April 25, 1898. Despite the grave attracting many visitors and being featured in *Ripley's Believe It or Not!*, that is all we know about Linnie Crouch. Due to some lazy engraver, we don't even know when she was born. This is of course very silly, as there are four perfectly good, if tiny sides to the gravestone that could have been used for additional information.

All we can deduce is that the small size was probably not due to a lack of money; the engraving is well made with a bit of style to it and has a decorative border. Also the cemetery is well maintained to this day and was never used as a pauper's burial ground. So this tiny bit of rock leaves us with many more questions than answers; for example, was Linnie tiny? Could she possibly have been the smallest woman ever? Because that would be awesome.

Another close contender for smallest tombstone is one that we actually do know something about. In 1929, the *Milwaukee Sentinel* reported that an Indiana cemetery had what they thought was the world's smallest, at 4 by 2 by 7. Reading only "Chase, the Barber," it marked the grave of Charles M. Chase, who, perhaps not surprisingly, had been the local barber for many years, although it does suggest an abnormal devotion to his career. Can you imagine someone inscribing, "Jason, the IT Consultant" on his gravestone today? Adding to the obsession theory, according to the paper, is the fact that during his lifetime Chase had used the small stone to prop open the door of his business. It was probably only a matter of time after his death before his friends discovered his hair collection . . .

**A GRAVE IS A PLACE WHERE THE DEAD ARE LAID TO AWAIT THE COMING OF THE MEDICAL STUDENT.**

AMBROSE BIERCE, WRITER (DIED 1913)

# THE LARGEST TOMBSTONE IN THE WORLD

You might expect some ancient king to have built a giant tombstone to himself, and many of them did make sure monuments went up recording all their achievements. But those monuments usually weren't the actual slab over their grave. The largest tombstone that was not a statue or otherwise some sort of monument, may have belonged to one Henry Scarlett of Upton, Georgia. While no records of his grave appear to exist today, from 1888 (when he was supposedly buried) until about 1890, his huge tombstone was covered by a dozen major newspapers including the *New York Times*. Considering the fact that these same newspapers were reporting bat-men living on the moon and UFO sightings around the same time, we do have to take the story with a grain of salt about the size of his alleged gravestone. However, if it did exist today, it would be hard to miss, as Scarlett apparently selected a mound of granite that was 100 feet by 250 feet and had it professionally engraved with his vital information (minus his date of death) while still alive. Instead of trying to move the huge stone, he had a tomb excavated underneath it. Locals reported that Scarlett had always been a bit weird and that, while he donated a lot of money to charity and other good causes, he lived like a hermit. Some attributed this to a woman breaking his heart in his youth. If true, this adds a real Freudian touch to the giant rock; after a life of celibacy his balls must have felt that large.

# THE MOST VIOLENT FUNERAL

They say you can't take it with you, but "they" were obviously never supreme rulers of millions of people. Now, the best thing about being an absolute ruler is that you don't just get to take material possessions with you when you die, you also get to force a whole bunch of people to come with you as well. Some great rulers took as many as a few hundred servants with them to the afterlife, but Genghis Khan took this practice to a completely new level when he died.

***Now, the best thing about being an absolute ruler is that you don't just get to take material possessions with you when you die, you also get to force a whole bunch of people to come with you as well.***

Genghis Khan had risen from a difficult and impoverished childhood to unite hundreds of tribes and slaughter his way across Asia, creating the greatest empire the world had ever seen in the process. Then when he was sixty-five he fell off his horse and died, a decidedly lame ending for such a badass. While his death was sudden, he had prepared for it in advance. As well as having already divided his empire among his sons, Genghis had picked out a spot to be buried. However, like many great generals he died on campaign far away from his preferred burial site. This wasn't a problem; according to Marco Polo, the Italian explorer who spent more than twenty years in China, the Mongols were used to carrying their deceased leaders' bodies for up to a hundred days in order to bury them. But Genghis Khan had asked that his gravesite be kept a complete secret, so the procession was going to have to take some drastic measures.

To start, they didn't tell anyone that Genghis had actually kicked the bucket before they started the long trek to the place he had picked out. Along the way the soldiers escorting the body made sure to kill anyone who happened along the procession. To put that in perspective, many historians believe Khan died in Egypt, meaning the procession had to walk 4,000 miles to Mongolia in order to get to the burial site. But if you were some random Egyptian peasant who saw the procession as it passed your farm, you were pretty much dead. They were not taking any chances.

Once they got to the burial site, slaves built an appropriate tomb. We have no idea what it looked like, although historians think a recently discovered fresco may depict the Khan's funeral. Showing an ornate tomb and coffin, it indicates that many hundreds of slaves would have been needed to complete it. However, they weren't given much time to admire their craftsmanship. Once they finished the undoubtedly detailed and ornate work fit for such a great ruler, the soldiers thanked them by killing them all. Then they buried their ruler, along with the 2,000 additional recently slaughtered servants he might need in the afterlife. Right after the funeral the soldiers killed everyone who had watched the burial, be they monks, government ministers, or random passersby. And, just to be absolutely sure that no Mongolian Dr. Doolittle would try to find out where the grave was, all the animals in the area were killed as well, including at least forty horses.

Of course, the 800 soldiers doing all this killing in the name of Genghis's privacy also knew where the grave was located. So after they took care of everyone and everything else they were also killed, although who exactly did these final killings isn't recorded. While this may have been quite literally overkill, Genghis got what he wanted. Almost immediately people had no idea where the Mongols' greatest ruler was buried, and to this day archaeologists spend their careers searching for it. While it might seem like a long shot, they might want to be careful of any murder-obsessed soldier ghosts, who would probably manage to find a way to keep that place hidden even if it means scaring a few thousand more people to death.

# THE MOST EXPENSIVE FUNERAL

These days the mortuary business is a billion-dollar industry, thanks mostly to the fact that it is really hard to take a few weeks to bargain shop when you have a dead body that needs burying. But the cost of a funeral today is nothing compared to what used to be spent on someone's sendoff. Now, it's always hard to compare anything ancient to the modern day, but even with limitations like conversion rates and lack of information, historians agree that the most expensive funeral of all time—by miles—was for Alexander the Great. Considering Hollywood couldn't even make a terrible movie about the guy for less than $155 million, you know everything in his life (and death) must have been over the top.

Alex was off fighting, expanding his empire, and having affairs with his bodyguards when he kicked the bucket. No one is quite sure how the great general died, but theories include:

- Poisoning
- Typhoid fever
- Liver disease
- Overeating
- The flu
- Malaria
- Leukemia
- West Nile fever

What we do know is that Alexander was far from home when he suddenly took ill and died after a long night of partying. This presented the first problem for his subordinates (other than the whole dying thing). Alexander died in present-day Iraq, but his body would need to be buried 1,800 miles away in his home country of Macedonia. And since he was such an important leader, plans would have to be put in place for a grand procession the entire way back; they couldn't just dump his body in the river and claim he was abducted by aliens, although that would have been much easier for everyone involved. There was no way this was going to be done quickly or on the cheap.

In the end it took two years just to get everything organized. In the meantime, depending on your sources, Alexander's body was either mummified by Egyptian embalmers or preserved in a vat of honey. Had they combined the two options and added some spice they could have had a honey dry mustard–glazed leader, which could have been delicious—if the Greeks had been cannibals of course. Finally, everything was ready. The historian Diodorus describes in detail how they tarted the body up like a parade float. First Alexander was placed in a gold sarcophagus filled with expensive spices and incense. This was in turn placed in a gold casket. Then the whole kit and caboodle was covered with expensive purple cloth woven with gold thread. In case things weren't gaudy enough just yet, everything was then placed in a gigantic golden chariot, studded with precious stones, and covered with golden animal carvings and garlands. To make sure no one missed the enormous shining carriage followed by hundreds of people, a large bell was attached and rung constantly so that everyone would know how important the guy inside was. Either that or they would quite rightly assume they were watching the world's first gay pride parade.

Of course, even with two years of preparation, the best laid plans of mice and men and all that. Despite an expensive tomb being built for him in Macedonia, Alexander's remains never made it home. One of his generals hijacked the procession and took it to Egypt. There he had another huge tomb built for his late ruler that included an ornate glass sarcophagus so that people could come to view the honey glazed body for the next 500 years or so.

In the end, Alexander's entire funeral is estimated to have cost $600 million in today's money. That means that, as a tourist attraction, the tomb would have needed to take in almost $1 million a year just to break even on the funeral costs more than half a millennium later. And for a while it might have seemed like a good investment, but as early as A.D. 400, writers were commenting on the fact that no one knew where one of the greatest rulers in history was buried. Money well spent.

# THE LARGEST COFFIN

Since people are getting larger, it follows that coffins are getting bigger, too. But no matter how morbidly obese society gets, there is a good chance that no one will ever have use for the largest coffin in the world—hopefully!

At 66 feet long and 20 feet wide, the giant wooden coffin in Truskavets, Ukraine, is actually used as a death-themed restaurant. Called "Eternity," the menu has themed meals named after local burial customs (most of which don't translate well, but do include "Let's meet in paradise." It probably also includes the famous "double coronary bypass burger," "kill-all-the-French fries," and pumpkin pie. Strychnine seasoning is optional).

The interior of the restaurant is decorated with actual funeral paraphernalia, including regular-sized coffins still in their plastic wrap, wreaths, and solitary candles. While it undoubtedly adds to the ambiance, the decorations mean the restaurant also serves as a storage space, since the owners operate their own funeral home just down the road. Perhaps too optimistically they hope that the record-breaking coffin will draw tourists to their city. The same way a seafood restaurant may hope the biggest lobster in their aquarium may draw diners in.

**IF THIS IS DYING, THEN I DON'T THINK MUCH OF IT.**

LYTTON STRACHEY, WRITER AND CRITIC (DIED 1932)

# THE LONGEST FUNERAL PROCESSION

Unlike coffins, other funeral items are hard to make bigger and bigger. Hearses, for example, can only be so large before they become unruly to drive. However, bringing hearses together to make one long hearse parade is a surprisingly hard-fought record in the short time since the *Guinness Book of World Records* created it. In 2011, two separate groups, one in California, one in Michigan, both attempted to bring together the fifty hearses needed for the record. It was not the Michigan group's first attempt; the year before they had managed forty-three. (Of course, the dedication of the members of "Just Hearse 'N Around" might have something to do with the fact that they are located in and around a town called Hell.) However, their perseverance paid off, and on their second attempt they set the first record with fifty privately owned hearses and one funeral director participating. Their happiness was short-lived though, as within months a group of funeral directors in the Netherlands topped them with a 107-car parade. The thoughts of accidental observers were not recorded, but we can only assume they thought a Mafia family reunion didn't go as planned.

Just Hearse 'N Around tried to surpass that number again in 2012, but could only drum up sixty-six hearses and a flower car. Again it was mostly private owners participating, with organizers saying that the lack of support from business owners may be down to the fact that they take a "dim view of recreational hearse owners." In other words, if you own a hearse to do your job, that is fine, but if you own one for fun you are a bit weird. After all, you're not making any money, freak.

## THE MOST VISITED CEMETERY

If you were lucky enough to die in Paris sometime in the last 200 years, there is only one place you wanted to be buried—the Père Lachaise Cemetery. A home after death for hundreds of the great and the good, this cemetery is one of the most popular tourist attractions in the capitol and is reputed to be the most visited cemetery in the world. Hundreds of thousands of people walk through its extensive grounds every year, while in their graves the impossibly posh dead people most likely look down their noses at the riffraff invading their space.

Napoleon opened the cemetery in 1804, saying it should be open to people of all classes and backgrounds. To prove his point the first person buried there was a five-year-old girl who came from a poor family. But Napoleon also wanted important people to get interested in being buried there, so he made sure that the child had famous neighbors, including the bodies of the long-deceased playwright Moliere and famous star-crossed lovers Abelard and Heloise, who were quickly moved from their original resting places to the new cemetery to increase its cool factor.

The marketing strategy worked and within twenty-five years there were 33,000 people buried in the posh new cemetery. Famous residents include rock star Jim Morrison; composer Frédéric Chopin; mime artist Marcel Marceau; singer Édith Piaf; artist Camille Pissarro; and authors Marcel Proust, Oscar Wilde, and Gertrude Stein, just to name a few. If there was ever a cemetery that you'd wanted to be haunted it would be this one.

***Famous residents include rock star Jim Morrison; composer Frédéric Chopin; mime artist Marcel Marceau; singer Édith Piaf; artist Camille Pissarro; and authors Marcel Proust, Oscar Wilde,***

***and Gertrude Stein, just to name a few. If there was ever a cemetery that you'd want to be haunted it would be this one.***

You can still be buried in the cemetery today, but even if you are young and healthy you will want to request a space now. The waiting list is extremely long and space is limited. If your permanent home isn't in Paris you will also have to make sure you at least die in the city or you do not qualify for burial in the Père Lachaise, meaning it is much easier to get into the most exclusive clubs in Paris while alive than it is to get into the world's most popular cemetery when dead, though seemingly not cheaper.

Even if you do manage to snag a space, don't expect to have that grave forever. Like other overcrowded graveyards, older bodies are routinely removed to make room for newer ones. Purchasing a burial plot is extremely expensive in the cemetery, and most people choose to pay for the 10–15 year rental options. Others even rent their grave for up to thirty years, hoping that their descendants will continue to foot the bill for their prime real estate. Once your time is up your bones are moved into the giant ossuary. While there are only 70,000 graves, official estimates state that anywhere from 1 to 3 million people have been buried in the cemetery at some point in the past 200 years.

# THE MOST EXPENSIVE HEARSE

In 2012, Rolls Royce decided to corner the market in recently deceased car enthusiasts for whom money is really no object (a group made up of literally tens of people) by introducing an unbelievably expensive hearse to carry them to their final resting place. While the coffin-mobile doesn't have an official price yet, the company says it is unlikely to be under $662,000, meaning you could almost afford two regular upper-end Rolls Royce's in life before you could in death. Launched at the mortuary world's biggest event, the Tanexpo, this super hearse's unveiling brought some class, excitement, and most importantly, news coverage, to what is normally most likely a dour three-day affair. (By the way, the Tanexpo? Way to rub it in on all of the people who are never going to see sunlight again.)

The company that outdid themselves with the Rolls Royce, Biemme Special Cars is an Italian company that specialized in taking regular cars and modifying them to fit a large wooden box in the back. In the past they created hearses based on expensive Mercedes-Benzes and other sports cars, but they really went above and beyond with the Rolls. First of all, the model they chose for their base design is called the Phantom. Let that sink in for a minute. It was either an intentional joke on the company's part or something was seriously lost in translation. Then there was the decision to keep the four-door styling of the original; the two rear doors open backwards and are colloquially known as suicide doors, adding to the array of inside jokes the mortuary business apparently uses to keep things light. If you own a funeral home, just remember to keep all this in mind before dropping more than half a million dollars on this piece of equipment.

It's not that you don't get a lot for your money. The car itself is a whopping 23 feet long, and is made from 600 different parts.

The 6.75-liter, 543-horsepower Rolls Royce engine is there, as well as its air-leveling suspension. So at least you know your last ride is going to be really smooth. The hearse is pretty beautiful, as hearses go, with large windows and an aluminum finish. But there is a danger in losing it, since, given the option, most car thieves—at least those who aren't opposed to jacking a hearse—would probably pick a Rolls over your standard Lincoln or Cadillac. The good news is that a seven-and-a-half-yard-long car stands out, so they would most likely be caught pretty quickly.

If you are looking for something a bit sportier, don't worry. There are options out there. After his death in a plane crash in 2010, the Polish president Lech Kaczynski was driven to his final resting place in a modified Maserati Quattroporte. Considering the fact that the Italian car company only makes three models, it was pretty much that or a convertible hearse.

**I DO NOT FEAR DEATH. I HAD BEEN DEAD FOR BILLIONS AND BILLIONS OF YEARS BEFORE I WAS BORN, AND HAD NOT SUFFERED THE SLIGHTEST INCONVENIENCE FROM IT.**

MARK TWAIN, AUTHOR (DIED 1910)

# THE CLASSIEST PET BURIAL

George Gordon Byron, sixth Baron Byron, more commonly known as the libertine poet Lord Byron, was a bit odd about animals. He kept a veritable menagerie throughout his life, including while he was at Cambridge University. When informed that dorm rules prohibited him from keeping any tame animals in his room, he retaliated by keeping a wild bear. The chance of being mauled to death was obviously a small price to pay for making a point. Byron owned more bears during his life, as well as various parrots, cats, monkeys, and a crocodile, just to name a few. (To be fair, he also had a thing for women, reportedly sleeping with more than 200 in just two years.) But above all, he had a fondness for dogs.

***When informed that dorm rules prohibited him from keeping any tame animals in his room, he retaliated by keeping a wild bear. The chance of being mauled to death was obviously a small price to pay for making a point.***

One of Byron's dogs, a Newfoundland puppy named Boatswain, became his favorite pet of all. The poet commissioned a portrait of the dog and took him everywhere. Then, at the age of five, Boatswain was bitten by a rabid dog and started showing symptoms of the disease himself. Lord Byron refused to face the truth, and when his beloved pet foamed at the mouth he would wipe it away with his own hands. When the dog finally died in 1808, Byron was apoplectic with grief. His friends knew that when he was affected by an idea he became obsessed with it, and with the death of Boatswain he took mourning a pet to new levels. Today we would just call him a drama queen.

First he wrote to his friends of his anguish, saying, "Boatswain is dead! . . . I have lost everything." Then he penned a twenty-six-line poem about the dog, which included the lines:

> . . . the poor dog, in life the firmest friend,
> The first to welcome, foremost to defend,
> Whose honest heart is still his master's own,
> Who labors, fights, lives, breathes for him alone,
> Unhonored falls, unnoticed all his worth,
> Denied in heaven the soul he held on earth . . .

Not exactly subtle. Despite protestations from his friends, Byron, already seriously in debt, spent lavishly on a large marble tomb topped by an urn for Boatswain's final resting place, his poem engraved on the side. It would be the only change he ever made to Newstead Abbey, the home he had inherited. Creaking floorboards and drafty rooms he could deal with, but dog graves were serious business.

Three years later, by which time most rational people have simply bought a new pet and moved on, Byron's love for his dead dog had not waned. The crypt housing Boatswain's remains was large for a reason. When Byron drew up his will he insisted, against the advice of his lawyers, that he be entombed there as well. As a gesture of thanks to one of his servants, Joe Murray, he offered him the honor of joining them. While Murray was okay with the idea of spending eternity beside his employer, he was less excited about sharing the space with a dog.

Sadly, Byron never got the chance to be reunited with Boatswain. He was forced to sell the Abbey a few years later, and when he died in 1842 the new owners of the estate were not keen to have him interred there. Even Westminster Abbey's Poet's Corner was off limits to him, thanks to his reputation as being "mad, bad and dangerous to know." (It might also have had something to do with the rumor that he had slept with his sister.) Instead he was placed in his family vault. By the early 1900s people started asking why one of the greatest poets in English history did not at least have a memorial in his honor in Westminster Abbey, and *Ripley's Believe It or Not!* pointed out in a 1950 issue that the poet's dog had a marvelous tomb while Byron did not. It was not until 1969, 145 years after his death, that he got a memorial as grand as the one he had made for his beloved pet, proving once and for all that it is not a good idea to sleep with your sister.

## THE MOST IMPORTANT FUNERAL

If you can judge how big a deal someone's death is by how many big names are at his or her funeral, there is no competition: Pope John Paul II had the most important funeral of all time. The pope had more world leaders at his funeral than Winston Churchill and more heads of state than had ever been in one place besides the United Nations. Almost every country in the world sent at least one representative, the most notable exception being China, which was not invited. That's a serious slap in the face when you consider that even the mass murderer (and current President of Zimbabwe) Robert Mugabe was at the funeral. The Orthodox, Protestant, and Jewish religions each sent numerous representatives. Prince Charles even delayed his wedding to Camilla Parker-Bowles in order to attend . . . but most people in his situation probably would have looked for any excuse to do the same. All told, at least 200 world leaders attended. While not the largest funeral of all time, the 4 million mourners who packed St. Peter's Square probably made it the largest Christian gathering in history, even bigger than the one in your local mall on Black Friday.

As soon as the pope died, the ring with which he sealed his official documents was removed and smashed in front of witnesses, so that no one could forge documents in his name. The last thing the church wants is a document "discovered" a few years down the line saying His Holiness thought birth control should be given out like candy. His personal rooms were sealed off, thanks to past cardinals who took the opportunity of a pope's death to loot his stuff.

While popes have been embalmed in the past, John Paul II was not, which may have been a personal choice. He might have heard stories of the disastrous embalming of Pope Pius XII in 1948, after which the corpse turned black and crumbled as it was laid out for viewing. The smell was so bad that the guards protecting the body had to be relieved of duty every ten minutes or they would be sick. Not surprisingly, the body was buried earlier than planned. John Paul's body started giving in to the elements by the time he was buried, but no viewers were reported to have thrown up, so it was a definite improvement. The people of Poland requested that the heart be removed from his body for burial in his home country, but the removal of internal organs had been illegal for popes for almost 100 years and was not allowed. This also means that any Italians who got a new kidney right after the pope died can't go around claiming they are infallible.

After six days the viewing of the pope's body ended and the funeral service commenced, broadcast to millions of people around the world. After the three-hour ceremony a small group of cardinals and friends of the pope attended the actual burial inside St. Peter's Basilica. The pope's simple wooden coffin was placed inside one of zinc, which was in turn placed inside one of carved walnut. Burial space in the Vatican is tight, with 263 other popes taking up much of the space, so John Paul's grave was a hand-me-down, originally used by Pope John XXIII, whose body had been moved after his beatification in 2000. While some popes were placed in ornate tombs, John Paul asked for a very simple one, covered with a stone slab. He got his wish for a few years, but his body has now also been removed in preparation for his expected sainthood, after which he will almost certainly get a fancier resting place. It just goes to show that even when you can draw bigger names to your funeral than anyone else in history, people stop caring about what you wanted once you've been dead long enough.

## THE OLDEST CEMETERY

In Matthew 24, Jesus has a rest on the Mount of Olives in Jerusalem and tells his disciples about the signs of the end times that doomsday predictors have been interpreting to no avail ever since. He also stood on this mountain when he wept over Jerusalem, was betrayed at the base of it in the Garden of Gethsemane, and ascended into heaven from it according to the Bible. So, for obvious reasons the mountain is a pretty important place for Christians. But this wouldn't be a typical site in Israel if it wasn't important to at least three different religions that were all fighting over it.

The Jews laid claim to the Mount of Olives 1,000 years before Jesus was born. Thanks to its location slightly outside the ancient city of Jerusalem and its easily yielding chalky soil, the mount made a perfect burial ground. Over the millennia the cemetery grew to house anywhere from 150,000 to 300,000 graves, with barely room to walk between them. Some of the oldest graves are actually impressive tombs traditionally associated with some of the biblical prophets like Haggai, Zechariah, and Malachi. One reason the site remained such a popular burial site was the prediction by the Old Testament prophet Zechariah that when the Messiah comes at the end times he will land on the Mount of Olives and split it in half. Since, according to the Bible, the dead will also be raised up at this time, getting buried on the mount meant you would be right in the middle of the action.

Unfortunately the giant cemetery has not been treated with the respect you would normally expect of a holy burial site for centuries now. Because of its height, the mount was a perfect spot for invading armies (and there were so very many of them over the years) to post troops and have a good view of the surrounding areas. By the 1850s, a nearby town was donating money every year in an attempt to maintain the integrity of the graves, but their charity proved futile.

The largest destruction occurred between 1948 and 1967 when the mount was under Jordanian rule. King Hussein (who you might have guessed was decidedly not Jewish) approved extensive building on the ancient cemetery, including roads, a hotel, army barracks, and a gas station. Some gravestones were reportedly used as free building materials. In 1967, Israel recaptured east Jerusalem and the mount, an action eventually condemned by the UN. Regardless, burials resumed in the cemetery and added yet another layer to the daily international incident that is the Middle East.

Due to the tensions rife in the region, desecration of the graves continues to this day. Tombstones are smashed, and mourners visiting the cemetery have been attacked. Since 2006, about $13 million a year has been devoted to restoring and protecting the graves. However, policing the 74-acre site twenty-four hours a day is proving impossible, as you might expect. But the good news is this ancient cemetery's problems should be fixed just as soon as peace comes to the country. Any day now, surely.

**I CAN'T DIE.**
**IT WOULD RUIN MY IMAGE.**

JACK LALANNE, FITNESS EXPERT (DIED 2011)

# THE LEAST DIGNIFIED FUNERAL

William the Conqueror did well for himself. Despite being born a bastard in a time when that sort of thing was a pretty big deal, he managed to work his way up in society, inheriting his father's dukedom in France and eventually invading England and making himself king there. But unlike the funerals of monarchs today, which are approached with utmost attention to detail and reflect the respect their positions entitle them to, William's funeral was a complete farce.

To begin with, even his death wasn't very dignified. At fifty-nine years of age, he was getting a bit old to be riding around on battlefields like a young knight. But he took to the saddle to put down yet another uprising in 1087, and lived to regret it, if only for a short amount of time. His horse spooked and William, who was by this point exceedingly fat, was thrown into the horn of his saddle. According to most historians this injury ruptured something internally and he passed away shortly afterward.

William died in France, so it was determined he should be buried there. But his sons and most of his lords ran off to secure their inheritances as soon as he died, so there weren't really any important people around to make decisions about his funeral. Finally someone suggested he be taken to Caen and buried in the Abbaye-aux-Hommes, which William himself had built years before as penance for pissing off the pope.

The funeral started out fine. Sure, no family was there, but nobody made a big deal about it. Then the bishop got to the part of the funeral service where he asks that anyone who had been wronged by William in his lifetime forgive him out of the kindness of his heart. One member of the congregation stood up and announced that William had stolen the land he built the church on from his father and he wanted payment before the king could be buried there. The service was halted while the dignitaries pooled enough cash to get this random guy to shut up.

Finally it came time to bury William. Unfortunately, this was before bodies in Europe were embalmed, and it had been just long enough since he died for William's already large body to start bloating. When his coffin refused to close, the men tried to force it, which resulted in the late king's body literally exploding. The stench was so bad that everyone ran for the exits, and the bishop performing the service basically speed-read the rest of it to get out of there as fast as he could.

Eventually they laid poor William to rest, but his body wasn't done with suffering indignities. It was dug up and examined at least once in the next few centuries, before being reinterred. Then in the 1500s a Protestant mob dug him up again and scattered his remains. Someone managed to recover the king's thigh bone, so if you go to France and see the impressive slab covering William's grave, just know that is the only bit left in there.

# THE FUTURE OF FUNERALS

These days technology is invading death almost as quickly as it's integrating into your life and soon it won't just be your phone and tablet you need to update every three months to stay relevant. You want to bring your gadgets with you to the grave? No problem. Think it would be cool to have people access your Facebook page on your electronic tombstone? Done. And if you are an environmentalist who wants to eschew traditional burial methods for something more Mother Nature friendly, you might think that you are selecting the greenest possible burial but rest assured in a short while someone will come up with an even better way to make sure your death doesn't cause any strain on the earth. No matter how green or advanced you think you're being when you plan your funeral, within a couple years you will be just as outdated as you were in life.

## SWIMMING WITH THE FISHES

If you want your ashes scattered in the ocean but still like the idea of your relatives being able to come visit from time to time, the Neptune Memorial Reef could be just the thing for you. Originally conceived as a re-creation of the fabled lost city of Atlantis, the creators realized they needed a way to keep cash flowing in while they developed their vision. Getting people to pay to be included as part of the underwater ambiance worked out perfectly. Apparently, the Death economy is always solvent.

The city is currently laid out as a traditional cemetery, although the builders expect to add more parts, eventually making this the largest manmade reef in the world. The cement columns, gates, and statues give an otherworldly look to the site, and the underwater cemetery has already been photographed for *National Geographic*.

If you want to have your ashes included in this underwater world, here's what happens: after cremation your remains are mixed with special cement that will not degrade quickly. The cement can be formed into any shape you want, although size and complexity will affect the cost. Some people have elected for a flat slab with a plaque that looks like a regular tombstone, while others have gone for more nautical themed shapes like a seashell. The most expensive memorials are the lion statues guarding the "gates" to the cemetery. Basically, your wish is their command when it comes to your burial marker—as long as the price is right. Once the cement containing your remains has dried a diver takes you down and adds you to the site.

While only about 300 people have been added to the "city" so far, the creators say there is room for 125,000 people, which would put it on the larger side as far as memorial parks go. And while visiting the site off the coast of Florida might be nice for some people, it would require quite a lot of friends and relatives to learn how to scuba dive first. Currently far more tourists than mourners are visiting the site. While dives only run about $80, joining the location permanently costs around two grand.

And if you are worried about the environmental impact, the Department of Environmental Resource Management already did a study on the young reefs and concluded that not only was it not hurting the area, it was actually helping it by providing living areas for species that haven't been seen in the area for years. Coral is already starting to grow on the columns and memorials, and various sea creatures are making the reef their home. And, as an added bonus, there will of course be some very confused paleontologists a few million years from now.

# WHEN SOCIAL DEATH MEETS ACTUAL DEATH

As video games get more immersive, players are forging deep connections with people on the other side of the planet. This is especially true when it comes to massive multiplayer online role-playing games (MMORPGs), games like *World of Warcraft* (WoW), where your entire gaming experience is heightened by the people you meet online. In most cases these individuals never meet outside of their computer fantasy world, but might spend hours every week chatting and going on quests together. This sort of a time investment makes the people who meet in these virtual environments feel it appropriate to hold a funeral if a team member dies. Since traveling across the country or around the world to the official, real-life funeral is probably out of the question, what better way to celebrate the life of their online friend than in the game where they all met and got to know each other?

That's exactly what one WoW guild (a group of players who meet online to complete tasks together) thought when one of their members unexpectedly died of a stroke in 2006. They organized an in-game funeral ceremony to commemorate their late friend (or her avatar, since that is what technically "died" in the game). Even though the event was taking place in a video game, the participants took it as seriously as a regular funeral and hoped that others would respect the solemn occasion.

***Even though the event was taking place in a video game, the participants took it as seriously as a regular funeral and hoped that others would respect the solemn occasion.*** ***This is where you have to wonder if these people really understood the mentality of the Internet.***

This is where you have to wonder if these people really understood the mentality of the Internet. Their first mistake was to hold the funeral in a setting that allowed people to virtually attack and kill them. They had other options, so this was a huge oversight. Pretty much everyone knows that people on the Internet aren't always exactly respectful about death—kind of like the Mafia. So, when word leaked out about their planned funeral a rival guild called "Serenity Now" decided to crash the funeral and kill everyone—also like the Mafia. One of the participants recorded the raid and the seven minute video is online to this day.

While Serenity Now technically didn't break any rules—after all the game is largely about fighting other players—WoW forums blew up with people asking if what they did was socially acceptable. Opinion was divided, with many people saying the guild throwing the funeral should have known what would happen. Whatever their opinion, everyone learned their lesson. While e-funerals still occur in online games, none have reported being raided during the event. If enough safeguards are set in place, virtual funerals could be the way of the future, with all your relatives having their own avatar and crying over a digital coffin. So much for the canapés at the wake.

# COFFINS AND COMPUTERS

For people who like both technology and death paraphernalia, computers and coffins form a natural Venn diagram. So it should come as no surprise that geeks are combining the two in both life and death.

That's right, you don't even need to be close to death (even if your social life was DOA a long time ago) before you get all the benefits of a computer coffin. One tech-savvy individual used his talents to convert a full-sized coffin into a case for his PC. The white casket when closed hardly looks different than a regular coffin, apart from the wires sticking out of the side. But open the head end of the coffin and you'll find a monitor embedded into the lid itself. The bottom half of the casket houses the computer itself, and when turned on the large cross cutout glows orange. The most difficult moderation was probably the keyboard tray, which had to be cut out of the bottom of the coffin. Now, this isn't the most practical case model in the world considering you need a six- or seven-foot-long desk that can handle a decent amount of weight. And if the guy who created it ever did manage to get a girl home, the large coffin in his room would probably put her off (unless he was Robert Pattison and the whole thing was sparkly). However, if you don't want to go whole hog and have a life-sized coffin, you can add just a hint of the macabre with two-foot-tall speakers shaped like coffins. While not available in stores, that hasn't stopped some anonymous Internet users from modifying their own speakers like this. It appears that when it comes to technology, death is a popular theme. And Goth kids and trust funds also form a natural Venn diagram.

But what about when you die? Do you have to give up computers forever? Of course not. If we have learned anything, nothing is beyond taste when it comes to the afterlife. When William Alan Watson died in 2009 at the age of fifty-seven, his brother decided that the computer nerd deserved to spend eternity in one of his beloved machines. It helped that Watson had been cremated. His brother gutted an old SPARCstation computer and made sure all the holes were plugged. At Watson's memorial service people wrote their goodbyes on Post-its and slipped them through the floppy disc slot. A plaque was added with Watson's name, dates, and the quote, "Beam me up, Scotty. I'm done here." Apparently Watson had quoted Star Trek shortly before he died, perhaps hoping he would wake up in an episode, which means that the whole computer thing makes a lot more sense. The computer-urn was so successful that despite their original plans to bury it, Watson's daughters reportedly started reconsidering their decision. Not least since it stood out from other funeral "reboots."

**I GET MY DAILY PAPER, LOOK AT THE OBITUARIES PAGE AND IF I'M NOT THERE I CARRY ON AS USUAL.**

PATRICK MOORE, ASTRONOMER

# DIAMONDS ARE FOREVER

They say a diamond is a girl's best friend, but now that saying applies both figuratively and literally. You see, when you get right down to it, people are made mostly of carbon, just like those precious stones, so it makes sense that some entrepreneur came up with the idea of taking cremated human remains and turning them into actual diamonds. Creepy? Yes. Fascinating? Absolutely!

In 2002 a Chicago company called LifeGem announced that they had perfected the process to create high-quality gems out of the cremated remains of your dearly beloved. These aren't "real" diamonds in the sense that they weren't formed underground after hundreds of thousands of years of natural heat and pressure, but these days, synthetic diamonds, ones not made out of recently deceased people, are almost as common in jewelry stores as their mined counterparts. So the technology to form diamonds out of the dead wasn't that far behind.

And, the dead don't even have to have died recently in order for you to have a pair of earrings or a nice stud in your watch face. In 2007 LifeGem took a 200-year-old lock of hair from Ludwig van Beethoven himself and extracted some of the carbon, then used it to grow a half-carat blue diamond. The company put it on eBay and asked $1 million for it, a pretty ridiculous price for such a tiny diamond, no matter who it is technically made out of. At least all the money was being given to charity. In the end the stone sold for a song at just over $200,000.

***In 2007 LifeGem took a 200-year-old lock of hair from Ludwig van Beethoven himself and extracted some of the carbon, then used it to grow a half-carat blue diamond. The company put it on eBay and asked $1 million for it . . .***

One of the reasons buyers might have been wary, and why anyone looking to turn their granny into a set of diamond studs should also be concerned, is that there is no way to conclusively tell that a diamond came from a certain person. While LifeGem and the half dozen similar companies that sprung up since its inception have never had any complaints about the quality of their products, the fact is that people are paying hugely marked-up prices for rocks that could just be the same type of synthetic diamonds you could buy in any jewelry store. Still, if you are willing to take the risk, for a little as $4,000 you can wear a tiny piece of your dearly departed for the rest of your life. If you're really into the idea, LifeGem also offers to turn your cremated pets into diamonds. People are obviously interested, as the company's profits are increasing every year and they have been covered everywhere from newspapers to *The Today Show*. After all, diamonds are forever—and so can be your antisocial pet.

# ENVIRONMENTAL EXPIRATION

Just a few decades ago many people's goal in life was to make a mark on the world, but these days people are increasingly trying to not only make sure that their existence doesn't make any sort of an impact whatsoever on the Earth, but that they metaphorically turn the lights off behind them as they leave it. How to cater to the eco-minded? Enter the eco-coffin.

Obviously, burials are not the most environmentally friendly way of leaving the planet, especially if your body is full of embalming fluid and your coffin is made of lead-lined processed wood. Super green coffins allow people to have traditional burials while barely making a scratch on the environment. Thousands of people in Europe and North America are now requesting green burials, including actress Lynn Redgrave and the founder of the Body Shop, Anita Roddick, and the numbers are increasing exponentially.

Carpenter Peter Lindquist of Maine was first turned on to eco-coffins accidently during his high school shop class. While trying to come up with something to make for his grandmother (who he must have thought had literally everything else already) he decided on the gift every healthy sixty-five-year-old woman would love: a coffin. Yes, he gave his grandmother a coffin on her birthday. The project took him the whole year, and his grandmother eventually accepted it with good humor, and she proved she still liked it twenty-seven years later by using it when she died at age ninety-two. Now Lindquist makes simple pine coffins for people who want to be buried in unprocessed local wood.

In England they have taken the eco-coffin a step further. After all, using any wood whatsoever requires cutting down trees. You know what is 100 percent environmentally sound? Wool. Not only do no sheep die, the popularity of wool coffins may just be the thing that saves the failing wool industry in Britain. The caskets are made from the wool of up to three sheep and are completely biodegradable. Most companies do not even dye them, which makes the coffins even greener. They can also be made in any size, hold up to 900 pounds, and cost a fraction of what bespoke oversized wooden coffins cost. Considering the Brits began their worldwide conquest on the back of wool in 1699 by making all their colonies, including America, buy wool from the motherland, we could be looking at a morbid return of the British Empire—via coffins.

In addition, many companies are also looking to less labor-intensive materials for green burials. Cardboard coffins have become popular, but they do have the rather unfortunate problem of sometimes collapsing before the deceased is actually in the ground—sometimes during the funeral itself. Other companies make coffins out of recycled newspapers, which not only allows for a sturdier build, but adds to the green effect by recycling up to 120 old papers. Gives new meaning to reduce, reuse, recycle, doesn't it?

**EVERYBODY HAS GOT TO DIE BUT I HAVE ALWAYS BELIEVED AN EXCEPTION WOULD BE MADE IN MY CASE.**

WILLIAM SAROYAN, WRITER (DIED 1981)

# THE ORGANIC AFTERLIFE

For some people even being buried in completely eco-friendly coffins is doing too little for the environment. After all, no matter what they're buried in, decomposing bodies let off a lot of carbon dioxide, and plenty of that is affecting our ozone already. And while one body is unlikely to make any difference, some people are concerned enough to shell out for some pretty futuristic ways to dispose of their corpses.

## PROMESSION

The first is called Promession. Invented by Swedish biologist Susanne Wiigh-Mäsak in 2005, this process involves literally shaking a dead body to pieces. Of course, there is more to it, or intestines would be flying everywhere. First the naked body is submerged in a vat of liquid nitrogen and its temperature reduced to 200 degrees below zero. The process takes up to two hours, and by that point the body is frozen enough to shatter easily —like, in less than a minute. Then the corpse is vibrated until all that remains is a fine powder—and any dental fillings. These fillings, the bane of the cremation industry because they don't burn down but still release mercury into the atmosphere, are still a problem in Promession and they need to be removed from the remains with magnets.

Once the body has been reduced to a pile of powder, it is put in a box made of something super organic like potato or cornstarch. From there is it usually buried in a shallow grave with a tree planted on top. The addition of plants is important in organic burials, since it represents the whole *Lion King* Circle of Life thing. This process has proved so popular in Sweden that the inventor received an award from the king himself, and other countries have expressed interest in their own Promession centers. While it might sound like something out of a Bond villain's playbook,

Wiigh-Mäsak insists that the process is "quite pleasant." We presume she means for the corpse . . .

### RESOMATION

If you are looking for something even greener, but with slightly grosser results, look no further than the process of resomation. At first it doesn't seem that different from Promession, with a body placed in a simple silk bag and submerged in a liquid. But this liquid is made from lye and water, and instead of freezing, the body is effectively boiled with the temperature reaching 320 degrees. When the process is finished about three hours later the bones are still intact but are usually crushed into a powder and returned to the family. The rest of the body isn't necessarily something that relatives are going to want to hold on to: by then everything else has been reduced to brown "goo." But hey, anything for the environment, right?

# DEAD DOGGY DUPLICATION

By this point it is probably clear that people care just as much, if not more, about what happens to their pets after death than any other loved one. And while cloning of human beings brings to mind the horrible dystopian futures that Hollywood is so fond of portraying, no one seems to have blinked an eye at cloning pets. Which means, of course, that people with more money than sense have spent tens, in some cases hundreds, of thousands of dollars to get exact genetic replicas of their deceased pets. Clearly none of these patrons has read *Pet Sematary*! (Everyone knows that there *are* nonevil pets waiting patiently in shelters hoping to be adopted, right? Just checking.)

It won't surprise you that many of the first people to clone their pets named their "new" pets completely unoriginal names. The first commercially cloned pet was a kitten, Little Nicky, who was made from the DNA of the late Maine Coon cat named Nicky. Nicky's owner, a woman from Texas who refused to release her last name, paid $50,000 to a South Korean company to give her the closest thing to having her beloved pet back. While she insisted it was worth it, and that the personalities of the two cats were virtually similar, her decision drew the ire of animal welfare groups who tried to explain to the public what that money could have done for cats that already existed and needed homes. To be fair, Nicky's owner probably spent the same amount of money on haircuts and manicures that year.

More pet cloning quickly followed. There were five different clones of a dog named Booger for a man from California. Then Double Trouble, a clone of a Lhasa apso named, of course, Trouble. Trouble's owner had already paid for a giant mural of Trouble's face to be painted on her apartment wall, so the fact that cloning him cost $50k and she was out of work at the time obviously was not going to be a problem in her mind. Not all pet clonings are so cheap though. A Labrador named Lancelot cost his owners $155,000 to clone. Part of the difference in cost is how hard it is to get a viable clone. Lancelot took eighty-four embryos in five different moms before he worked out.

While cloned pets may act very similar to their predecessors (or at least their owners may be convinced they do) one of the main questions cloned pet owners face is, "Why don't they look the same?" Dogs can have floppy ears when their clone had straight up ones, and cats can be completely different colors entirely from their original. The fact is that regardless of the starting genetic "blueprint," during gestation an animal will grow in a unique way. Unless you have ultimate power over every atom and molecule in the developing creature, that is. In which case you may as well skip the whole cloning process and start whipping us up some sweet dinosaur-sharks.

**Die? I should say not, dear fellow. No Barrymore would allow such a conventional thing to happen to him.**

John Barrymore, actor (died 1942)

# GO OUT WITH A BANG

On August 20, 2005, a slew of celebrities gathered for the funeral of writer Hunter S. Thompson. He had shot himself earlier that year at the age sixty-seven and left detailed plans for his funeral. He was to be cremated and his ashes loaded into a cannon on top of a large specially designed pillar. His rich friends, including the actor Johnny Depp, made sure this odd sendoff happened exactly as Thompson requested. As his ashes were shot into the air, fireworks went off behind the cannon. While the Gonzo author was probably the only person in history ever to go out this way, funerals and fireworks are not mutually exclusive. Unlike Thompson, though, most people who have mini Fourth of July celebrations at their sendoffs are actually in the fireworks themselves.

Numerous firework companies advertise the fact that they will pack the remains of your loved ones into tiny rockets and explode them in a dazzling display. Even more companies seem to be open to the idea when it is specifically requested. But Heaven's Above Fireworks in the UK is a company dedicated specifically to memorial firework displays, most of which include at least part of the deceased. And if you don't want to pay for a complete display you can also get "self-fired" pyrotechnics you can fire off at home, allowing the deceased to be a part of literally every Guy Fawkes Night celebration for decades. And yes, the company will also make fireworks out of your late pets.

Even if you haven't had a loved one pass away recently, your local Fourth of July firework spectacular might not be as corpse free as you would expect. One celebration in Florida, which was watched by over 200 people, included the cremated remains of Tom Moore, whose wife said it was an appropriate sendoff and that her husband would have loved "going out with a bang." In Indiana in 2008 a town honored Meredith Smith, the man who had started their fireworks celebration forty years earlier, by including him in the explosions. Smith solicited donations for the first town fireworks display and continued to put them on himself for over four decades. When he died at the age of seventy-four his wife requested that some of his ashes be used in that year's celebration, seeing it as the only fitting tribute to his memory. While her children were initially skeptical, they eventually agreed, and the family got together to fill the rockets up themselves. They even printed up special celebratory T-shirts marking the occasion. Bet those got a lot of use after the big sendoff . . .

# ART IS DEAD

Last we checked there wasn't exactly a shortage of paint or clay in the world, but that hasn't stopped modern artists from always looking for the next controversial thing and experimenting with different media. One of the weirdest is the use of human ash in art. More than one contemporary artist has decided that the best way to imbue their work with personal meaning is to add an actual person to the mix, literally.

Two companies with names so similar they actually have disclaimers about not being the other one on their websites, Art from Ashes and Art in Ashes, use very small amounts of the cremated remains of dead friends and relatives to make paintings and jewelry. The national media have featured both companies, and the idea seems to be growing. While these companies' pieces tend to be rather traditional, other than the added remains obviously, other artists are going completely out there.

Daniel Ortega of Arizona makes abstract, mixed-media works that he feels really get an added boost from ashes. At first he added things like coffee and dried goat poop, but then a very creepy idea came to him. Many vet offices cremate animals that they euthanize and the owners don't come to pick up the remains. So he started calling around to vets and asking if he could have the ashes for some artwork. Eventually he started including the remains of animals that people wanted to remember, and charged up to $1,000 a piece for them. But what he really wanted to do was move into human remains, so he offered a free painting for the first person to send him a loved one's ashes. Unlike the two companies mentioned above, who use a nominal amount of ash, Ortega uses up a couple pounds of the remains. But don't worry, you will get back whatever amount he doesn't use of your loved one, and Ortega promises he has "never dropped any ashes on the ground." At least not yet . . .

The artist Wieki Somers went a step further, combining cutting-edge technology as well as ashes and art, when she used a 3-D printer to make sculptures of a toaster, a vacuum, and a scale from human ash. Each of her three pieces was made from the remains of a single person, commemorated on the front with a plaque. By making items we usually think nothing of replacing when we are done with them, out of something so important as human remains, Somers wanted to examine the lengths we would have to go to in order to be personally attached to everyday objects. Because that's not creepy . . .

**Life is pleasant. Death is peaceful. It's the transition that's troublesome.**

Isaac Asimov, author (died 1992)

# THE VERY COLD HAND OF DEATH

Cryonics or cryopreservation, sometimes wrongly called cryogenics, is the process of putting a recently deceased body through a "freezing" process in the hope that the person can be revived in the future. While most scientists agree that this wish is as about as realistic as wishing on a unicorn, the slim possibility of owning an iPhone 27 (complete with hoverboard technology) is enough for some people to invest tens of thousands of dollars in the technology.

As well as being one of the most well-worn science fiction tropes, the idea of being in some sort of suspended animation for decades in order to see what the future will be like has been a dream of mankind for a long time. Even Benjamin Franklin wrote that he wished such technology existed in his time so he could see what would be going on with the United States in a hundred years, which considering it was Franklin, would probably just mean boning women in different style dresses than he was used to.

It wasn't until the 1960s that the technology finally caught up with the idea. In 1967 the first man, Dr. James Bedford, was frozen and even made headlines for a very short time, until the 100 percent for certain deaths of three Apollo astronauts kicked him off the front pages. It turns out that tragic American hero deaths make better stories than mad scientist deaths. Go figure!

However, people were slowly getting more interested in the possibilities of cryonics when, in 1979, seven bodies were accidently unfrozen. This set back the technology years, because the chance of waking up during the Carter administration was enough to frighten off even true believers. In the 1980s some widely publicized court cases led to cryopreservation becoming a legal alternative to cremation or burial across the United States. More recently, the government has shown interest in the process, hoping that advances in the science might one day allow humans to enter suspended animation and travel deep into our galaxy. And then bone some aliens, obviously.

Only about 250 people have been frozen after death since the technology became available, most famously baseball player Ted Williams (the rumor that Walt Disney had his body frozen is an urban legend). The main problem is the cost. Since no one knows how long it will be until humans advance far enough to not only unfreeze bodies but revive them and fix whatever ails them, money is needed to pay for storage for at least a century or two, just to be on the safe side. You need to have the money ahead of time, because there is a chance that your heirs won't want to spend thousands of dollars of their inheritance keeping a slightly bonkers great-grandparent in cold storage. Some companies charge up to a quarter of a million dollars for the procedure.

If you are a bit short of cash but want to take another chance, you can always just store your head. People who do this are only out about ten grand, but they are counting on our descendents being able to upload thoughts into a computer or at least hoping that they can join a bunch of celebrities in a head museum one day, a la *Futurama*.

Still, if you are going to go to all that trouble just to wake up confused and alone in a couple hundred years, you will want to have a furry friend with you. One cryogenics institute in Michigan houses almost as many pets as it does people. Although if you have ever given a dog a bath, you can just imagine what a pitiful site they will be after they are unfrozen.

**IT'S NOT THAT I'M AFRAID TO DIE. I JUST DON'T WANT TO BE THERE WHEN IT HAPPENS.**

WOODY ALLEN, DIRECTOR AND ACTOR

## RENEWABLE ENERGY—CREMATION STYLE

In 2008, one crematorium in a small town in Sweden failed an environmental test; their cooling towers were no longer up to code and would have to be replaced, an expensive and time-consuming process. Instead of just writing a check and getting on with it, the owners started talking about the intersection between cremation and environmentalism and they came up with a crazy idea. The heat and smoke from the ovens was not only being wasted, but it cost money and required energy to cool down before releasing it into the atmosphere (this is more important in Sweden than other countries, because the resulting rise in local air temperature from "icicle nipples" to "barely livable" would mean that the land around crematoriums became the most expensive places to live). What if there was a greener way? What if instead of letting off that heat, they used it to warm the crematorium and cemetery buildings? Their speculation may very well be the way of the future. But if you live in a handful of towns in Europe, you are already enjoying a warm house partially thanks to your recently deceased neighbors.

> ***[I]f you live in a handful of towns in Europe, you are already enjoying a warm house partially thanks to your recently deceased neighbors.***

The problem is that burning a body is a strain on the environment. It uses a lot of gas during the actual immolation process, but the smoke is worse. Because we all hate flossing, most people have fillings, and when they burn they release mercury into the atmosphere. This has to be filtered out before the smoke can be released or people living in the surrounding area will suffer from something called "death." The smoke also has to be cooled down drastically.

It starts out at about 2,000 degrees and most countries require water cooling to get it down to 150 degrees before it is acceptable for the atmosphere, a technique that is always so successful for nuclear power plants. A crematorium meltdown might be a lot less radioactive, but do you really want to be able to make ash-angels in someone's grandma?

By redirecting the smoke and turning it into a power source, crematoriums are able to reduce the amount of energy they use while reducing the power usage of the people who receive the green energy. Everyone wins! The reaction has been surprisingly positive to what could be a very controversial idea. Sweden's test run worked so well that a few towns in Denmark also went the dead-bodies-as-fuel route. So many large crematoriums participated that they actually sold the resulting energy to the national grid, rather than directly to a few consumers. Some towns in England have recently considered the scheme, with one already using power generated from crematorium heat to warm their local swimming pool, saving the local council more than $20,000 a year. In all of these towns the locals have been polled about their feelings on the subject, and the overwhelming majority has reacted favorably.

While it may be in its beginning stages, some countries with extremely high cremation rates, like Japan, may find that harnessing the power of the dead may be a huge step to lowering their carbon footprint while, ironically, making more carbon. Fight fire with fire!

# WOEBEGONE WEBCASTS

It used to be that if someone died whom you were particularly close to (or at least if you were named in the person's will) you dropped everything to attend the funeral. It didn't matter if this involved driving for hours, paying last-minute fares for flights, or taking time off work without pay. You had this one chance to grieve with everyone, and you were expected to be there. Seriously, swim oceans, crawl through hot lava, the point is be at the church on time or be forever known as the one in the family who didn't care enough to show their face at their great-uncle's funeral. At least the exhaustion and jet lag should make it easier to cry.

Enter technology. Like almost everything else these days, the Internet has made attending funerals so much easier. It had to happen eventually. After all, no one thinks it is weird if you can't make an important birthday party and arrange a Skype call instead; even weddings are being broadcast on the Internet in larger numbers, with a streaming option now available in many venues. But there was something about funerals that made them more important to attend in person. It was the last celebration to fall to the ease of the modern world, but just like present-day Luddites who fear the rise of the e-book, one day people will look a bit odd for not mourning remotely.

Big funeral events like Michael Jackson's memorial have led the way in making saying your last goodbyes online more acceptable. Now more and more funeral homes are offering the service, with many seeing the number of clients taking them up on the offer increasing tenfold in the past few years. In many cases, far more people watch the funeral online than attend in person. The on-demand option is even more popular, with those who couldn't watch live choosing to view the ceremony at a later time, because we are now at a place in our lives where we demand so much convenience that we won't even mourn our family members live if it interferes with an episode of *Mad Men*. Many people say they watch the services more than once, as a way to deal with their grief and reflect on different aspects of the ritual. With that in mind, network television might want to start broadcasting a couple reality shows about funerals. *How I Met Your Undertaker*, *Desperate Widows*, and *Survivor: Not Really* can only help at this point.

Not all funeral home owners are happy with these new developments, however. Some balk at them for being untraditional, others see this as the demise of the funeral in general. But services geared toward the online audience tend to be much more about a celebration of life and concentrate less on the bod, which in turn makes the whole funeral experience a lot less creepy. Some warn, however, that eventually the physical funeral will become unnecessary, as the role of the deceased's remains becomes secondary to online guest books and memorial videos. At that point, we might as well go back to mass graves and save a couple thousands of dollars.

If you want to check out a funeral webcast but no one you know has recently died, just check out some funeral home websites, like the Conley Funeral Home or the Bailey Family Funeral Home. While most offer password protection on their streamed services, just like with their wireless connection, most people don't bother to set it up, meaning that absolutely anyone can mourn a complete stranger from halfway around the globe. Ah! The miracle of technology!

**I HAVE NEVER KILLED A MAN, BUT I HAVE READ MANY OBITUARIES WITH GREAT PLEASURE.**

CLARENCE DARROW, LAWYER (DIED 1938)

# FAT FUNERALS

While many companies are concentrating on the fun, technological, and futuristic innovations for the mortuary industry, the real money might be in finding a way to deal with our rapidly expanding waistlines. More than one-third of Americans are classified as clinically obese and the number is growing, with 50 percent of the population projected to be seriously overweight by 2030. So now we have turned to the same marketing techniques that got us here in the first place and started ordering our funeral stuff "supersized."

Back when people didn't drive around parking lots for ten minutes trying to find a spot 15 feet closer to the entrance, coffins came in 24-inch widths; now the standard is 27 inches. Even that is not nearly large enough for many of our more rotund dearly departed anymore. Some funeral homes now also supply "oversize" caskets up to 52 inches wide, which might also be a cheaper way to go if you ever know some thin identical twins that die on the same day. Of course, with a bigger casket comes a bigger burial plot. While some cemeteries are starting to sell wider plots, many require customers to buy two plots next to each other to accommodate the larger coffins, meaning the same indignity that larger people suffered on airplanes when forced to buy two seats follows them to the grave.

There are also safety concerns. Even regular coffins aren't very light, and larger caskets, once full, may not be able to be carried by funeral staff. In addition, unless bodybuilders start switching careers in droves, heavier caskets can require special loading equipment and hearses, already much longer and heavier than your average car, cannot handle the extra weight. In some areas this has meant a return to horse-drawn funeral carts that can be made quicker and cheaper, and are designed specially to carry heavier loads. With all the more complex and specialty aspects in mind, a supersized funeral can end up costing $3,000 more than one for an "average"-sized person. If you think the comments your skinny sister makes when you have a third helping at Thanksgiving are bad, you do not want to know what she will say once she finds that out. Fortunately, by that time you won't actually be able to hear her.

Cremations add a whole new world of problems. Fat burns at a much higher heat than the rest of the body, so the more fat involved the longer the cremation process takes. It also requires higher temperatures, which as one Austrian crematorium discovered in 2012, can actually be pretty dangerous. The immolation of a 440-pound woman caused the oven to burn so hot that the entire building caught on fire. Now both Austria and Switzerland are considering weight limits for cremations in their countries. Cremating larger bodies also released too much carbon dioxide into the air, causing otherwise up-to-code crematoriums to fail environmental compliance checks. Once we've gotten to the point that our fatness is ruining the ozone layer even after we die, it might be time to start eating some vegetables. Or you could just say screw it and finish that bag of chips—after all, it won't be your problem anymore . . .

# DIGITAL REMAINS

In the past you only had to worry about your (probably) eternally damned soul and, to a lesser extent, what happens to your body when you die. But these days people are seriously concerned about something in between the ethereal and the physical: their digital remains.

Think about it. When you die, will the right people know all of your passwords and have access to your accounts? Should you put that information in your will? Who gets ownership of your music collection, e-books, and domain names? Not surprisingly, companies are springing up to help people deal with all of these things and more. True, we could all just figure this stuff out for ourselves, but this is capitalism at work, damn it!

***When you die, will the right people know all of your passwords and have access to your accounts? Should you put that information in your will? Who gets ownership of your music collection, e-books, and domain names?***

Of course, it's not just about who gets what. There are also people you don't want seeing certain things. You might not mind if your brother finds your extensive porn collection, but what if your mother does? Well, these new companies will make sure (for $10 to $30 a year) that your digital information is stored and, when the time comes, they guarantee to distribute the information to the correct people. Just don't forget that you signed up. While some companies require two people to confirm your demise before they release the information, others require you to continue to prove you are still among the living at certain intervals, in some cases daily, or the information is sent out, which seems an awful lot like blackmailing you with your own life.

While it would be embarrassing enough to let people know all the secrets of your digital life once you are dead, you will never hear the end of the mockery about your Britney Spears playlist if it leaks while you are still alive.

But all these companies offer is storage. What if you want to stay connected all the way to the grave? That is where the eTomb comes in. This is an actual physical tombstone, but with some sexy information-age bells and whistles. Still in development, this special tombstone would contain all the online information about the deceased, their photos, Facebook page, and so on, and would allow people in the cemetery to access the information through Bluetooth devices. All of their digital information in one place would act as an Internet memorial to the deceased, and loved ones could send messages or post thoughts about them. You know how annoying it is to go to dinner when everyone around the table is poking at their smartphone? Now imagine that at a funeral (careful, too many tears can mess up your touchscreen). Solar panels built into the tombstone would keep it charged. Of course, it wouldn't be a true online experience if there weren't trolls, so the eTomb would also have safeguards ensuring that only nice things were posted in this virtual guestbook. All that would be required is for a grieving family member to go through and delete all the horrible messages people say about you.

Of course, the eTomb still requires the family member to be close to the grave for access. Many people have friends they only know online, or who live thousands of miles away. In those cases the Facebook pages and Twitter feeds of the deceased become their own memorials. In fact, almost all social networking sites have official policies regarding what happens to an account once someone dies. Your iTunes library reverts to Apple, something that some individuals are trying to fight in court. Facebook freezes your account in time and won't delete it (this has already lead to complaints that Facebook recommended people become friends with the recently deceased). Eventually the laws may catch up to the digital age, but you may very well be dead by then. It might be best to plan ahead—just leave your password in your will and hope your beneficiary won't pretend you came back from the grave.

# PLASTINATION

Since 1979, German Gunther von Hagens has been perfecting his plastination technique for preserving body parts. As a medical student von Hagens was inspired both by medical models that encased specimens in plastic externally, and a ham slicer. That's right, he looked at a ham slicer and thought, you know, I should really figure out a way to preserve body parts from the inside. Weird? Yes, but at least it wasn't a meat grinder.

After some hits and misses, von Hagens came up with a process that worked and patented his idea in Germany and the United States. The key was to remove all the parts of the body that lead to decomposition, namely fat and water. By replacing them with liquid polymer in a complex, multistep process, the breakdown of remains can be virtually halted. At first von Hagens mostly used it on animal parts for veterinary schools and small human parts for medical study. But in the 1990s he decided to go all out and try to preserve full human bodies. The results were so extraordinary that von Hagens put together a show of whole bodies in Japan in 1995. More than 3 million people attended. Since then his Body Worlds exhibitions have become some of the most popular and controversial showings at museums all over the world. While ostensibly for people to learn about different aspects of human anatomy, the shock factor is a huge reason people turn out to see the macabre exhibits.

These days there are more than 400 labs in forty countries working on preserving human parts from the inside with plastics. The best examples and advances in the technology are highlighted at an international conference every two years. With so many new specimens, the obvious question is just where are these body parts coming from? Von Hagens promises that all of his work comes from people who left their bodies to his company. Since he first started about 9,000 people have signed up—yes, you too could become a giant plastic GI Joe!—with around 90 percent of those people hailing from Germany. But should the number of willing subjects ever dry up, he also maintains that the scientific advantage of his work outweighs any need for specific consent, so if you die in Germany just hope your plastic pose is a good one. Von Hagens also sells some of his work through an online store. Despite the fact that there is probably a disturbingly sizable part of the population who would pay good money for well-preserved human remains, as a conversation starter/centerpiece at fancy dinner parties, plastinations are only available to "qualified buyers," individuals or institutions who will only use them for medical research. Guess that's something to hang your hat on!

**DIE, V.: TO STOP SINNING SUDDENLY.**

ELBERT HUBBARD, ARTIST (DIED 1915)

# STUFFING MAN'S BEST FRIEND

Everything old is eventually new again and one death-related fad starting to come back in a big way is having your pets professionally stuffed after they die. Like so many of our very odd funeral traditions, we have the Victorians to thank for starting this tradition. In the 1800s pet ownership among the middle and upper classes soared. Unwilling to let go of their beloved animals, many owners had them stuffed and placed around the house. The practice eventually became so popular that *Punch*, the preeminent satirical magazine of the day, produced a weekly comic devoted solely to making fun of the bad workmanship and lifeless appearance of most of the animals. Much like a modern day celebrity magazine, but with pets.

These days taxidermy technology has moved on, and there are now dozens of companies out there vying for the right to preserve your deceased pet. If you ever watched *Scrubs* and thought that the stuffed Labrador Rowdy was the best part of the show, now is the time to do your research. Documentaries on the subject exist, and in 2012 Animal Planet started broadcasting a TV show about a family-owned pet taxidermy service. While the idea may seem strange, enough people are interested in keeping the outer shell of their beloved pet around forever to support a diverse market. While some taxidermists specialize in cats and dogs, others receive requests for all kind of animals. The most important part is deciding how you want your pet posed for eternity; while curled up as if sleeping is most popular, people do ask for animals sitting up, eyes "open," and sometimes even action poses—permitting the longest game of fetch ever.

> ***The most important part [about taxidermy] is deciding how you want your pet posed for eternity; while curled up as if sleeping is most popular, people do ask for animals sitting up, eyes "open," and sometimes even action poses—permitting the longest game of fetch ever.***

Some stuffed pets are actually famous. The most famous dog in Japan was named Hachikō, an adorable Akita puppy that would greet his owner at the train station as he came home from work every day from 1923 to 1925, when his owner died. Although Hachikō would live ten more years, he never forgot his beloved human and would show up at the train station every day at the same time hoping to see him get off the train. (We'll wait while you go get some tissues.) He became a celebrity and a symbol of perfect loyalty in a country that was really big on that sort of thing. When the dog died he was stuffed and is still on display in Tokyo's National Museum of Nature and Science.

While Hachikō may have been gifted to the nation, one beloved stuffed pet was recently sold for a lot of money. Roy Rogers was a famous western star in the 1940s and '50s, and in most of his movies and television shows he rode his beloved horse Trigger. Trigger became famous in his own right, and when he died Rogers had his hide removed and professionally mounted in a rearing position. The horse was originally part of the Roy Rogers Museum, but when it closed in 2009, Trigger was sold at auction. A television station bought him for $266,500. It is unknown if the same fate was considered for Roy Rogers.

# CAN YOU HEAR ME NOW?

The world is so connected now that you can't even switch off when dead. In a serious technological one-upping of the Ouija board, funeral homes around the world are reporting an increasing number of people being buried with their cell phones. And why not? You worked for hours to get three stars on all those Angry Bird levels, there is no way you are leaving them behind.

In ancient Egypt the deceased were buried with things they might need in the next life, like some treasure and a few thousand slaves. These days the only thing anyone really needs to get along in the afterlife is a full battery and someone on this side of the veil to pay your phone bills. That's not a joke; at least one woman is still paying her late husband's Verizon bill more than four years after his death, all so she and her sons can continue leaving him messages about his favorite sports teams. She even invited the public to get in on the act by having his cell phone number etched on the gravestone. So if he is getting his voicemails in the great beyond, he's probably wondering why loving messages from his family are interspersed with prank calls from giggling teenagers.

Anecdotal evidence suggests this trend is especially popular with those who die young. One man was reportedly buried with his Bluetooth headset firmly in his ear, presumably because he wanted to be just as much of a douchebag in death as he had been in life. Another popular theme is to leave the phone's volume on loud and then call it as the coffin is lowered into the ground, which has the double benefit of literally saying goodbye to someone as you are seeing them for the last time, as well as scaring the shit out of unsuspecting gravediggers.

If you are one of the millions of people who plan on being cremated after you die, don't worry, you still don't have to give up your iPhone. Recently many caring, but slightly misguided, family members started slipping smartphones into the pockets of their gadget-obsessed loved ones right before they were placed in the furnace, a trend that became immediately obvious when the bodies started exploding in the fire. Now many crematorium owners offer to put the cell phones in the urn with the ashes in order to avoid any more unfortunate mishaps.

Of course, no new technological trend would be complete without pissing off some hippies. Despite having no official numbers for how many people are following this trend, some groups have raised concerns that while burying formaldehyde-filled corpses in lead-lined coffins is fine, cell phone batteries are a big environmental no-no. Fortunately, some companies are working on "green" cell phones, so even if you are concerned about your grandpa's carbon footprint you won't have to resort to paying a psychic to let him know the results of the Super Bowl.

**I HAVE NOTHING AGAINST UNDERTAKERS PERSONALLY. IT'S JUST THAT I WOULDN'T WANT ONE TO BURY MY SISTER.**

JESSICA MITFORD, POLITICAL ACTIVIST (DIED 1996)

# PRECAUTIONS FOR THE COMPLETELY PARANOID

There are hundreds, if not thousands of examples through history, as far back as records go up to the present day, of accidental premature burial. The thought of waking up from a coma to find oneself buried alive is enough to terrify even the most rational person, but most of us don't actively prepare for the possibility. The one exception is the still popular practice of having wakes, which were originally held just to make sure the deceased wasn't going to sit up. But some individuals have come up with incredibly creative ways to ensure that if they do happen to wake up six feet under, someone is definitely going to hear about it.

One of the most basic ways to ensure you were not subject to premature burial was to leave instructions in your will for someone to beat the crap out of your corpse. There were many recorded instances of "dead" bodies waking up on the dissection table, so by insisting that they be beaten, the fearful hoped it would answer the question of their mortality once and for all. Doctors usually charged extra to perform these grueling tasks, but people paid, and therefore we have records of people being impaled and beheaded before burial, just in case.

By the 1800s, newspapers in Europe were declaring that premature burials were at an all-time high. Whether true or not, it led to more advances in the "making sure you are dead" industry. One patent was filed for a coffin where a button was placed on the lid close to the chest. If the body started breathing without gaining consciousness their chest would push the button and set off an alarm in the cemetery's office. For tomb burials, coffins were fitted with springs so that any movement would cause the lid to spring open, something that must have made for a hilarious funeral mishap at some point. Some people buried in tombs also insisted on having a hammer and chisel so they could get out if no one heard their cries.

> ***Some people buried in tombs also insisted on having a hammer and chisel so they could get out if no one heard their cries.***

By far the most famous precaution involved being buried with a string tied to the finger, which rang a bell above the grave if the interred awoke. This was often used in conjunction with a breathing tube so you wouldn't suffocate before someone realized the ringing was a person come back to life and not just a lost cat. A variation on this was a box containing a flag, which would shoot out when the string was tugged on, indicating signs of life to those above—or alternatively being extremely helpful if the gravediggers ever decided to play cemetery golf.

Despite advances in medical technology, the fear of being buried alive still persists. In 1995 an Italian company started offering a casket/survival kit. Among the other amenities, it included an oxygen tank, defibrillator, and a two-way microphone allowing communication between the would-be corpse and the outside world. And while most people who take cell phones to the grave these days do it for symbolic reasons, there are areas where bringing a phone and numerous batteries "just in case" is popular, especially in South Africa.

Proponents of cremation have long been pointing out one of its most obvious benefits: it is impossible to be buried alive. Of course, you do risk being burned alive, so you really can't win either way.

# ASHES TO APOGEE

In 1994, NASA predicted that space burial would be a thriving industry by now, appealing mostly to science fiction fans and Buddhists from Japan because they "are very receptive to innovation and have a calmer approach to death than most Westerners." Of course they also predicted that by 2010 we would be treated in space hospitals, so their suppositions should be taken with a large grain of salt. But, despite some setbacks, space burial companies are trying to get a foothold in the billion-dollar mortuary industry.

Starting at about $1,000 and reaching up to fifteen times that, you too can shoot your earthly remains into space. Well, part of them anyway. A really small part. In fact one company refers to it as a "token amount," or about one gram of your ashes. You won't even be up there forever, depending on which package you choose; most of the cheaper options include being shot into a low earth orbit in a capsule with other remains. Since what is up must come down, the capsule falls back to Earth and burns up in the atmosphere after about a year. There have also been accidents. With space flight, sometimes things go wrong, and of the eight missions in the past fifteen years, two have failed.

On top of these serious limitations, it takes years before you can send your loved ones off into the wild blue yonder after they die. Even Majel Barrett, the wife of Star Trek creator Gene Roddenberry, who died in 2008, is not scheduled for launch until 2014. Rodenberry himself was one of twenty-four people whose remains were on the first space burial mission in 1997. Many of the people who have chosen this route were involved in space in some way during their lifetime, with a notable exception being the LSD-promoting college professor Timothy Leary, who, though he may have thought he was exploring outer space while under the effects of psychedelic drugs, never actually went.

For the time being, space burials are purely for humans, although the ashes of a police dog that died in 2008 may have been a stowaway on the same ship that carried Star Trek actor James "Scotty" Doohan's ashes. Only one person has been given the honor of having his ashes buried on the moon: the astronomer Dr. Eugene Shoemaker.

If the only thing stopping you from partaking in some afterlife spaceflight is the cost, all is not lost. States including Virginia and Florida are considering giving tax credits worth thousands of dollars to families whose loved one's remains are shot into space from their state. The goal is to get their foot in the door of space commerce, like a twenty-first Century Life Insurance salesman.

**SOME MEN ARE ALIVE SIMPLY BECAUSE IT IS AGAINST THE LAW TO KILL THEM.**

EDWARD W. HOWE, EDITOR (DIED 1937)

# CRAZY ONE-OFFS

Humans go to such efforts to convince themselves that death is something that just happens to other people that, when faced with the reality of it, some people fall off the deep end. For example, you may not think that some guys would take their friend's corpse out drinking, but it has happened. People seem to go especially crazy when it comes to stealing anything to do with dead people—from grave goods, to hearses, to the bodies themselves. Something about being around a corpse seems to turn otherwise normal people into kleptomaniacs. Of course sometimes it is the dead people themselves who can turn a funeral upside down, especially when it turns out they aren't dead. If you want to cause your relatives a bit of consternation even after death, why not take some tips from those who went before you: Crazy wills, funny tombstones, and requesting a clown at your funeral are all ways to keep everyone on their toes even after you are long gone.

# NIGHTMARE NAPTIME

While the fear of premature burial is enough to make people go a bit crazy, if the corpse manages to wake up at just the right time it can turn a funeral into a party. While it is hard to be completely certain about foreign reports of sudden life syndrome, the frequency with which they seem to occur is either awesome or concerning. Here are some from just the past two years:

## THE BEST NAP EVER

A ninety-five-year-old Chinese woman named Xiufeng Li decided that, despite her age, the Grim Reaper wasn't getting her yet. Unfortunately that is not how it looked to her neighbor, who stopped by and found her unresponsive on the floor of her home. Her body was put in an open coffin in her house for friends and relatives to come see. Imagine that same neighbor's shock when he came to pay his respects and found an empty coffin. Li had woken up after five days and was making herself something to eat. She declared she had had a lovely sleep, in the no-bullshit way only a ninety-five-year-old woman can.

## HOW TO MAKE A FUNERAL INTO A PARTY

A twenty-eight-year-old waiter in Egypt owes an observant doctor his life. After collapsing at work from a suspected heart attack the man was prepared for a quick burial, as Islam requires. The doctor sent to sign the death certificate at the funeral didn't like how warm the corpse felt and after a couple tests determined he was still alive. His mother fainted when she was told, but once everyone was revived the funeral turned into a "You're Alive" party (also popular in war zones).

## THE GRATEFUL NOT-DEAD

Mourners didn't respond so favorably during a Yemeni man's funeral. When the "corpse" was lowered into the grave he started shouting about how he was alive and they were going to kill him. The attendees, quite rightly, panicked but did eventually pull themselves together and rescue the would-be corpse from his own grave. In a similar incident, a man presumed dead and held in a morgue freezer in South Africa woke up after a few days and started screaming. The workers "thought it was a ghost and ran for their lives." The man was eventually rescued, cold but otherwise unharmed.

### CLOSE BUT NO CIGAR

Unfortunately, not all wakings have a happy ending. In Russia, a woman reportedly sat up during her funeral only to be so terrified that she suffered another heart attack and died . . . again. And a Brazilian boy who had apparently died of pneumonia sat up in his coffin during his funeral and asked his father for a glass of water. Sadly, even though the family started screaming that is was a miracle, the boy laid back down again and doctors who then examined him assured the parents that this time, for sure, their son was dead.

# MY PARENTS WENT TO A FUNERAL AND ALL THEY BROUGHT ME WAS THIS DUMB SKULL

Millions of years of evolution have managed to make our brains pretty clear on the fact that dead bodies are icky and are best left alone. Unfortunately, we are also obsessed with famous people and are pathological collectors of useless things. For some people, those last two manage to override any biological urge to get away from a corpse as fast as possible. Instead, some people look at part of a dead famous person and think, "I'm having some of that."

There are plenty examples of this practice in history, where the stolen parts are now lost to us forever. The mummified heart of Louis XIV was removed during the French Revolution, and eventually made it into the hands of an English minister who proceeded to eat it. Thomas Paine's entire body was dug up by a stranger and stored in an attic for years before being lost to history. And the Skull and Bones club, at the time led by Prescott Bush (father of President Bush Sr.), are accused of stealing the head of Geronimo during WWI and keeping it in their headquarters at Yale to this day.

But some bits of people who are otherwise happily buried are still around. The most famous is probably Albert Einstein's brain. Less than eight hours after he died his brain and eyes were removed during an autopsy. One could see how the great physicist, knowing his own extraordinary intelligence, would request his body parts be donated to science after he died, and it would be a beautiful story, except that isn't what he wanted at all. Einstein left specific instructions for the cremation of his remains. An autopsy wasn't even needed, as there is nothing suspicious about a seventy-six-year-old man dying after entering the hospital with severe chest pains. The pathologist on call that evening, a man named Thomas Harvey, just decided that Einstein's brain should obviously be studied, probably just before yelling "Yeah! Science!" along with repeated pelvic thrusts. When people found out the truth they were horrified, but it was too late. Harvey gave the eyes to a friend and kept the brain for himself, cutting it up into more than 200 tiny pieces. While scientists have studied the brain for more than half a century, they have yet to find anything that made it worth it.

The weirdest famous bit we have lying around today is actually someone's bits, that is to say, Napoleon's penis. While the provenance is a bit shakier than Einstein's brain, it appears that the ex-Emperor's penis was lobbed off during his autopsy, either accidently or secretly. The organ remained in the attending priest's family for decades until it was sold to an American as part of a lot of Napoleon's personal effects (although none obviously more personal than that). A few years later the penis was displayed without a hint of irony in New York's Museum of French Art. The media went mad for the organ, describing it in such unflattering terms as "looking like a maltreated strip of buckskin," a "shriveled eel," and "one inch long and resembling a grape." Well, we'll just see how your genitals look over a century after you've died, reporters. Shrinkage is probably a given with mummification.

# THE SADDEST SHAKEDOWNS

In the past, body snatchers digging up graves were usually looking for bodies the medical professionals would buy, so people might have thought their remains would be safe once they'd been embalmed or at least in the ground awhile. Not so much. If you are famous enough or if your relatives have enough money, even your decaying body can be worth big money. Criminals looking for a quick buck have attempted to ransom off remains for centuries.

## CHARLIE CHAPLIN AND TASSOS PAPADOPOULOS

Two months after Charlie Chaplin died in Switzerland two unemployed mechanics dug up his coffin and hid it. Believing that Chaplin's widow would pay anything to get her husband's body back, the body snatchers demanded a $600,000 ransom. Oona Chaplin flat-out refused, saying Charlie would never have wanted her to do such a thing. She did inform the police, however, and five weeks later the men were arrested and the actor's remains recovered. Just to make sure it never happened again, Oona had him encased in concrete. Still, Chaplin might not want to rest easy. In 2010, the body of the former president of Cypress, Tassos Papadopoulos, was stolen from his grave. In order to get to the body, the robbers had to move a 660-pound slab. While details of the crime were kept secret from the general public, they were told that it was a purely financial motive, not some extreme form of weightlifting.

## ENRICO CUCCIA

You may not like the Occupy Wall Street movement but you have to admit they have been really restrained when it comes to digging up the graves of rich bankers and demanding cash for their return, a common need many protesters face. A similar movement in Italy didn't show that type of restraint when, in 2012, it sent shock waves through the country by stealing the body of one Enrico Cuccia, basically the Warren Buffett of Italy. Rumors abounded about what crazy group had stolen the body, and the media speculated that it could be anyone from a satanic cult to the mafia (who were known to do that sort of thing in the past). Finally the police received a ransom note asking for $3.5 million in return for the banker. When the ransom wasn't paid immediately, the robbers called and demanded the money. The police put them on hold and managed to trace the call and arrive at their hideout before they hung up the phone. Cuccia's body was returned unharmed. Cuccia's son called the grave robbers crazy, although he seemed more confused by their choice of body, saying, "There are some much wealthier dead people." Unfortunately for him, *Forbes* doesn't publish such a list.

### ABRAHAM LINCOLN

Not all ransom attempts get off the ground, however. In 1876, a Chicago counterfeiter was sentenced to ten years in jail and his loyal and crazy friend hatched an audacious plan to get him released. They decided to steal the body of the late President Lincoln and demand $200,000 and a pardon for their friend. While today stealing a president's remains would be suicidal, not to mention virtually impossible, Lincoln was laid to rest in an unsealed sarcophagus, and his tomb was locked with a single pad lock. There was a very real chance his remains would have disappeared if the men had not invited a police informant to help them. Still, the would-be body snatchers actually got inside Lincoln's tomb before being scared away by the Secret Service.

## DINING WITH THE DEAD

It's probably not surprising that you should put off eating a hamburger until you are at least a couple hundred yards away from corpses, but this is not something that concerns the owners or patrons of the New Lucky Restaurant in India. The bustling café does good business selling tea and buns to customers who have to hop over graves to get to a table.

The restaurant started as a tea stall outside of a Muslim graveyard during the 1950s. After coming to pay respects to their deceased loved ones, mourners would then pay for some refreshments. Business was so good that the stall kept expanding, eventually coming right up to the edge of some graves. In a country where space is limited, when it came time to build a whole building there was only one thing to do. Rather than disturb the graves that were in the way, owner K. H. Mohammed simply built over them. Since the graves were partially above ground and surrounded by shin-high metal railings there was nothing to do but incorporate them into the floor layout.

Historians think the graves are up to 500 years old, so they are well taken care of. The current owner cleans them every day and places a dried flower on each. Some people even think the graves bring luck to the patrons, hence the café's name. However, new visitors might not feel so lucky, since the dozen graves are located in slightly inconvenient places and are a definite tripping hazard. The waiters, however, are pros at the fancy footwork needed to glide around the place, like some weird macabre ballet complete with refreshments at the end. The New Lucky remains popular to this day, with young couples seemingly particularly fond of the odd ambience. At night the tables and graves are lit by candlelight. Now what could be more romantic than that? And, even though the graves are Muslim, people say that the Hindu tradition of reincarnation makes being literally surrounded on all sides by death less creepy to Indians than it would be to Westerners. Be warned though—the dead never pay their bill.

**Death will be a great relief. No more interviews.**

Katharine Hepburn, actress (died 2003)

## URNS ARE SO OUTDATED

One of the benefits of cremation is that you can arrange for your ashes to literally become part of something you love. But while some might love art, space, or the ocean, others have slightly more bizarre ideas in mind for their remains.

### JAMES BOOTH

How about becoming an instrument of death? In 2004, Scottish native Joanna Booth lost her husband James after a severe case of food poisoning. Knowing her husband would want to go out with a literal bang, she came up with a very original idea for his ashes. James had been a vintage shotgun expert for Sotheby's auction house and was a gun collector and hunter himself. And since the stuff that goes in shotgun cartridges is a powder, and ashes are a powder, Joanna decided to ask a cartridge company if they wouldn't mind making a special blend just for her using the cremated remains of her late husband.

While a bit perplexed, the company agreed and produced 275 rounds of the special ammunition. In a further nod to her late husband's gun-toting days, Joanna then invited her husband's friends to come on a shoot, but not before having the shells blessed by a local minister. He agreed, calling the whole thing a "perfectly normal scattering of ashes." Normal must mean something different in Scotland, perhaps due to the abundance of whiskey. The hunting party brought down over 100 animals, including partridges, ducks, pheasants, and a fox. Clearly death ammunition is quite lethal. While her husband never actually asked to be memorialized in this way, his wife assured the local papers that he would have loved it.

## MARK GREUNWALD

One man whose tastes ran a little less bloodthirsty but no less weird was Mark Greunwald. When Mark died suddenly of a heart attack at age forty-three he had been working as a writer and editor at Marvel Comics for almost twenty years. Despite his young age, Mark had planned what he wanted done with his ashes, and somehow he got his wish. You see, he wanted to become a comic book himself by having his cremated remains mixed in with ink and printed in a comic that would actually be sold to the public.

Not surprisingly, Marvel took a lot of convincing. It wasn't until a year later in 1997 when they finally agreed to let Mark's widow mix his ashes into the ink that went on to be used in a 5,000 copy rerelease of one of Mark's old comics. While the ink long ago ran out, copies do show up for sale online from time to time. Just know that the guy who wrote the comic was way more into it than you and in a way is watching you enjoy it. Let's hope the folks over at *Playboy* don't get the same idea . . .

## LIKE TAKING CANDY FROM A CORPSE

Grave robbing isn't very common in the Western world anymore, but that doesn't mean that everyone has suddenly started respecting the dead. It just means that people have gotten lazier. Now when people steal from corpses they are much more likely to rob open caskets rather than putting in all that effort to dig one up. Part of the problem is that, as a culture, we haven't really moved on since the Egyptians and refuse to believe you can't take it with you; we still like to go to the great beyond with some of our most priceless belongings. Case in point?

Well, the funeral of Bradley McCombs was about as tragic as you could get. He was only seventeen when he died in a car crash on Christmas Day 2010. But his family was about to find out that things really could get worse. They had placed some of Bradley's favorite possessions in the coffin with him, including his Game Boy. Then the funeral home held a public visitation. Now, one would think the last thing to worry about with an open coffin would be some jackass stealing the Game Boy, but that is exactly what happened. A thirty-seven-year-old man was confronted by the family and eventually arrested after he stole numerous items right in front of everyone.

Game Boys might be a dime a dozen, but when Randall Joudan died his girlfriend knew he would want to go out with his $2,000 custom-made electric guitar. While the rest of his extensive and expensive guitar collection was displayed at his funeral, his Fender Telecaster was in the coffin with him, wrapped in his arms. It was too much for one guest, Steven Conrad, who decided the instrument was too nice to be in a crypt for eternity. How he managed to pry it out of the dead man's hands without anyone seeing is a mystery, but when he was eventually caught he said, "This isn't something I normally do. I just have a respect for fine musical instruments." A comment that was surely followed by him playing a wild rock solo. Obviously his love of music comes before any sort of basic respect for the dead.

And lest you think it is only at funeral homes that this sort of thing goes down, don't worry, just about everyone seems to be on the lookout for coffins to steal from. Airline workers charged with shipping a woman's body from Singapore to Mumbai took it upon themselves to open the coffin and steal all the jewelry the corpse was wearing, as well as $900. Why the dead woman needed the money is unclear, but the price of crossing the river Styx has probably gone up with inflation just like everything else.

***Why the dead woman needed the money is unclear, but the price of crossing the river Styx has probably gone up with inflation just like everything else.***

And while few people will dig up graves anymore, sometimes the treasures they know are there make it worth it. The New Jersey cemetery where Whitney Houston is buried had to hire twenty-four armed guards to keep an eye on her grave when word leaked that she was buried with $500,000 worth of jewelry. If she'd read her Egyptian history, she'd have known that she was just asking for it.

# COFFIN CONTESTS

No one likes to think about the fact that death is going to come one day, but the fact is we all will have to die, so why not grab a freebie on the way out? That's been the idea behind the various Win a Funeral contests over the years. There has almost always been an outcry about the tastelessness of such competitions, but really, is there anything more practical in the end?

In 1987, a Georgia newspaper, the *Free Lance-Star*, joined forces with a local funeral home to draw attention to drunk driving and hopefully save some lives by offering a free funeral to one not-so-lucky person. If people were willing to admit they planned on drinking and driving on New Year's Eve, and signed up at the newspaper office before the holiday, they could win a totally free funeral if their stupid decision actually did kill them. The newspaper assured readers that it hoped no one died but thought the contest would make people think about the realities of driving under the influence, ignoring the fact that the participants were effectively getting free life insurance for a boozy New Year's Eve topped off with a suicide drive.

The idea wasn't a one-off. The editor of the paper had been offering similar prizes at various publications for twenty years by that point. In 2007, a different editor at the *St. Mary's Today* in Maryland used a similar strategy to convince people of the seriousness of drunk driving, but the paper only offered a free coffin —not a whole funeral—to the first person to die while driving drunk over the holidays, so hopefully people weighed up their options pretty seriously on that one. After all, while coffins are expensive, they are not the bulk of the funeral cost so dying for one hardly seems worth it.

In 2011, a German radio station offered a prize of about $4,000 to the person who sent in the best epitaph. The only catch was the money had to be spent on death insurance which would eventually cover the winner's funeral. The submissions didn't have to be funny or even original, although the DJ admitted that would be preferable. The idea was to get younger people to start talking about the "taboo" subject, thinking about the realities of death and how it can occur at any time. Guess the Germans are real buzzkills . . . While a funeral director was actually sponsoring the contest, others in the mortuary profession didn't find the contest very funny. In particular, the Association of German Undertakers called the competition tasteless and even went so far as to file a lawsuit that eventually stopped the contest temporarily. While some people may have been uncomfortable with the idea, the radio station said that more than 600 people entered the contest, and the courts eventually upheld the legality of the giveaway.

**Dying is a very dull, dreary affair. And my advice to you is to have nothing whatever to do with it.**

W. Somerset Maugham, playwright and author (died 1965)

# GALLOWS HUMOR

While there are plenty of Photoshopped funny tombstones on the Internet, some of them do actually exist. For some people it is just a reflection of the sense of humor they had in their lifetime, for others a way for their family to get back at them. But they are all hilarious.

## SHOW BIZ TOMBSTONES

Jack Lemmon was typically self-depreciating when it came to his gravestone. It says, in its entirety, "Jack Lemmon in." The idea being of course that he is playing his last role, and doing it brilliantly and hilariously—as a corpse. Merv Griffin, most famous for creating *Jeopardy!* but also a talk show host in his own right, originally told people his epitaph would read "Stay Tuned" but before he died in 2007 seems to have changed his mind, as his grave actually reads, "I will not be back after this message." Mel Blanc, the voiceover artist famous for many *Looney Tunes* characters, had his most famous catchphrase, "That's All Folks" inscribed on his tombstone.

## OLD WEST TOMBSTONES

Gunfighters in the Old West also often had funny tombstones. The murderer Robert Clay Allison, who once allegedly survived a confrontation with Wyatt Earp, has two stones over his grave, the first insisting he was both a gentleman and a gunfighter, while the second makes a more succinct point, "He never killed a man that did not need killing."

## DEAD POETS SOCIETY

One of the most famous and yet also the most seemingly implausible of all hilarious tombstones is that of John Laird McCaffrey in the Notre-Dame-des-Neiges Cemetery in Montreal. At first glance the poem on his grave seems fine, if a bit trite:

JOHN,
FREE YOUR BODY AND SOUL
UNFOLD YOUR POWERFUL WINGS
CLIMB UP THE HIGHEST MOUNTAINS
KICK YOUR FEET UP IN THE AIR
YOU MAY NOW LIVE FOREVER
OR RETURN TO THIS EARTH
UNLESS YOU FEEL GOOD WHERE YOU ARE!
MISSED BY YOUR FRIENDS

It is only after looking harder that you might notice the message spelled out by the first letters of each line: John, Fuck You. Missed by your friends. While it seems like an Internet prank, the website Snopes has determined that it is in fact 100 percent real. A newspaper in Montreal even contacted the man who carved the stone and asked him about it. According to him he didn't notice the message until he was finished, but it made sense since the man's wife and mistress had ordered the stone together and said it "represented him." Just to lighten it up a bit they also requested a butterfly carving. It wasn't the first funny tombstone the man had been asked to carve either, a previous commission had said, "I'd rather be in Boston but my wife buried me here." Still, the Fuck You tombstone has to win for sheer creativity.

## CORPSE COUTURE

While dead bodies can be used for good, the problem is that the person who benefits is not the dead person—unless, of course, he or she is able to become RoboCop. It takes a pretty selfless person to let his or her body be destroyed in some way for the benefit of others after death. However, even if your attitude is "I'm dead, who cares?" if you lived in medieval Iceland, you would still have to be pretty magnanimous to help your friend out after death.

According to Icelandic witchcraft, the body of a dead man (it had to be a man, you'll see why) could help make someone rich. The key was getting permission from that man before he died, or the magic would not work. So you get permission from a friend, and then wait around for him to die. It isn't recorded, but presumably killing the person helping you out was also frowned upon. But hey, if you can get away with it . . .

Once your friend dies, let him be buried. Then one night before he starts rotting, go to the cemetery and dig him up. This is where the hard part comes in. You need to flay the skin from the bottom half of his body all in one piece. Rebury the body so no one notices that you just desecrated a corpse. Take the skin home and dry it out, then tan it like leather. Boom, you have your own awesome pair of skin pants. Since you are participating in witchcraft, and also because wearing human skin is frowned upon for everyone but serial killers, and even they barely get away with it, make sure you wear your new necropants under your regular pants. Now is the point where you turn all this disgusting work into something good, but first you need to do something else people usually frown on.

***You need to flay the skin from the bottom half of his body all in one piece. . . . Take the skin home***

***and dry it out, then tan it like leather. Boom, you have your own awesome pair of skin pants.***

Look around for a poor widow, the poorer the better. Then rob her. Not too much robbing; after all, she hardly has anything to steal, just make sure you get a coin. This is where the man part becomes important: place the coin in the little pouch of skin left by the scrotum. Add a bit of paper with the rune on it and watch as the ball sack of your magic pants fills up with money for as long as you keep them on, which should be every second for the rest of your life or the magic will fail.

When you realize you are going to die soon be sure to pass on the riches to someone else. To make your beneficiary's life easier you can actually gift them your skin pants instead of making them flay your dead body. As you take your leg out of one side have them slide theirs in. That way the pants are still being worn continuously. It's not documented exactly when this insane practice was realized to be about as profitable as milking a bull, but we can only assume the Icelandic people really needed something kinky to warm their cockles for this to be perpetuated for any length of time.

If you are now disappointed you were not alive in medieval Iceland, you can always go to the Museum of Witchcraft and Sorcery in Hólmavík and check out a replica pair of the pants for yourself. Just do the world a favor and have yourself committed afterward.

# LOVE AFTER DEATH

Elena Milagro de Hoyos (Helen to her friends) was just twenty-one-years-old when she contracted tuberculosis in 1931. Despite her loving family's best efforts—including all the money they spent for a supposed expert on the disease to treat her—she died. Helen was buried in a mausoleum that was kindly paid for by the nice German doctor who had failed to save her. Her family was obviously happy to have his help during that difficult time, but little did they know just how much Dr. Carl Tanzler loved their late daughter . . .

While treating Helen, the German-born Tanzler had fallen head over heels. He showered her with presents, including expensive jewelry. Sadly he was trained in radiology and was not the expert at treating tuberculosis that he pretended to be. When Helen died he shouldn't have been surprised, but he sure was distraught. After she was interred in the mausoleum he built for her he visited it almost every night. But eventually even this wasn't enough.

About eighteen months after Helen had been laid to rest Tanzler decided she needed to be moved. Obviously, the move wasn't just his decision; Tanzler claimed that Helen's ghost told him to take her body away to be with him. So he did. He broke into the tomb, carted off her body in the middle of the night, and took it to his house. He placed it in his bed, where he kept it for the next seven years.

***He broke into the tomb, carted off her body in the middle of the night, and took it to his house. He placed it in his bed, where he kept it for the next seven years.***

Of course, eighteen months after death Helen wasn't looking so great, but Tanzler did what he could to pretty her up. He gave the body glass eyes and used coat hangers to hold her bones together. As her chest had collapsed, he filled it with rags, and covered her decomposing skin with plaster. He even managed to get a wig made out of Helen's own hair to put on the corpse's head. He kept it immaculately dressed and used perfume, lots and lots of perfume, to try to keep away the smell. And every night he lay down next to his beloved, who looked more and more like a mannequin as the years went on.

He must have covered his tracks after he stole the body, because no one seemed to notice that Helen was missing. However, by 1940 rumors that he had her body in his house grew loud enough that her sister investigated. When the body was discovered Tanzler was arrested, but since the only crime he had committed was stealing a body and since the statute of limitations had expired he was released. The national media picked up on the story, but, shockingly, public sentiment was with Tanzler, who, instead of being seen as the obviously crazy man that he was, was portrayed as the ultimate hopeless romantic. The things people do for love . . .

# THE CADAVER SYNOD

These days, the College of Cardinals can elect a pope who used to be a member of the Hitler Youth and no one so much as bats an eyelash. But in the Middle Ages electing a pope was a vicious, sometimes deadly business. Popes were deposed, murdered, declared anti-popes after their death, anything just to get a different Italian ruling family on the papal throne. But in A.D. 897, Pope Stephen VII took his dislike of his predecessor to new levels when he convened what became known as the Cadaver Synod.

Pope Formosus wasn't the greatest pope in history, but he doesn't seem to have been terrible either. He didn't really have time to make his mark, since he only lived for five years after he ascended to the papacy. He just had the misfortune to be pope when Italy was in political turmoil—and one could argue that not much has changed in 1100 years. Still, it could have been worse; after Formosus died Pope Boniface VI lasted a whole fifteen days before he died. His sudden demise raised eyebrows, especially since the new-new pope, Pope Stephen VII, was about to prove he was a bit crazy.

About a year after Formosus's death, Stephen had him disinterred from his grave on Vatican Hill and brought to stand trial. Despite the fact that decomposition had set in Stephen had the corpse dressed in papal robes and seated on a throne. Since there was the obvious problem of a corpse not being able to defend itself in court, Stephen had someone stand behind the throne and "answer" the charges he brought against his predecessor. Formosus was accused of lying and cheating in order to become pope, as well as not ever having been ordained. If he were found guilty, this would mean all of the decisions he had made as pope would be null and void since he was never really pope to begin with. Shockingly the guy behind the chair didn't put up much of a defense and Formosus was convicted.

The corpse was stripped of its papal robes and had three of its fingers cut off. Stephen at first allowed it to be buried in a graveyard outside the Vatican, but then changed his mind and had poor Formosus dug up again and thrown in the Tiber River.

Formosus was vindicated though. Not only was his body recovered and eventually reinterred at the Vatican, but Stephen was deposed, thrown in jail, and eventually killed. Yet another synod was convened, this time thankfully without anyone's dead body on display, and all of Formosus's papal declarations revalidated. Just to make sure there wasn't an endless cycle of cadaver synods in the future, the cardinals also voted to make it against the rules to put a corpse on trial ever again. Took them long enough . . .

# THE FINE ART OF FAKING YOUR OWN DEATH

If there is one thing you learned in school it is that *Romeo and Juliet* is the most romantic story of all time. And what does Juliet do to solve all her problems so she can be with Romeo? She fakes her own death. Most people probably stopped reading at that point, but we're sure the ending proved that faking your death is a foolproof way of getting what you want.

In the real world people have gone to great lengths to fake their death for a variety of reasons, but usually it is to avoid a criminal charge, probably because going to all that effort just to get out of a blind date would be overkill. (Literally.) At least two people that we know about faked their deaths in the September 11 attacks, one to avoid prosecution for passport fraud and the other so her family could cash in on her life insurance policies.

## CONNIE FRANKLIN

In 1929, Connie Franklin tried to fake his death, and when he was eventually discovered alive and well, he found himself in the extremely odd position of testifying at his own murder trial. The accused man, on learning about Franklin's "death" had led the authorities to some remains, which he was then accused of creating. Since all evidence at the time pointed to them being Franklin's, his reappearance meant he was called as a defense witness, the defense being that he was very much alive and therefore the accused could not be convicted of killing him. As legal strategies go, that one is pretty much bulletproof.

## TIMOTHY DEXTER

Perhaps the saddest reason to fake your own death is to see how many people will show up at your funeral. That's right; the plot line employed by Ross on *Friends* well after the show had jumped the shark is something real people have actually attempted. The eighteenth-century eccentric Timothy Dexter was a popular author when he faked his own death in order to see how sad everyone would be when he died. While more than 3,000 people showed up for his wake, not all of them passed the test they had no idea they were even taking. His wife completely failed; while sitting by the coffin she remained stoic and did not cry. Franklin announced his survival by berating her in front of everyone for her lack of sympathy over his supposed demise. Considering how obviously bonkers her husband was, it's just surprising he didn't catch her dancing around the coffin yelling about how she was finally free.

### AMIR VEHABOVIC

In 2007, a forty-five-year-old Bosnian named Amir Vehabovic had the same idea as Dexter. But while Timothy may have at least gotten to enjoy some touching eulogies before he brought the service to a halt with his displeasure, Amir was angry right from the beginning. The whole point of faking his own death was to see how many people showed up at his funeral, so he was devastated when he got his answer—one person attended. His mother. Incensed, he wrote a letter to all his "friends" saying:

"I paid a lot of money to get a fake death certificate and bribe undertakers to deliver an empty coffin. I really thought a lot more of you, my so-called friends, would turn up to pay your last respects. It just goes to show who you can really count on."

Yes, who would have thought the sort of people who hang around with a guy who would fake his own death would be unreliable. Jerks.

# THE ONLY WAY FUNERALS COULD GET ANY WORSE

Just in case the act of attending a funeral wasn't disturbing enough, a company in Ireland is now offering a service absolutely no one asked for—clowns at funerals. That's right, someone thought taking the things that are so ubiquitously terrifying that Stephen King wrote a novel about them would really lift the atmosphere at an already slightly terrifying event.

While obviously the worst idea anyone has ever had in the history of the world, it actually does have precedent to back it up. The Romans, who, remember, had already added blood sport to their funerals, decided all that death was getting oppressive and that they needed something to lighten up the event. In their sick and twisted minds, the best way to get people laughing about their desperately missed dead relative was to hire a professional jester to dress up like the deceased. To take it a step further, the jester also wore a specially made mask in order to look like the dearly departed as well. Imagine showing up at your grandfather's funeral and seeing a guy wearing a Halloween mask standing over the coffin. While running for your life would be the logical reaction, this became a favorite part of Roman sendoffs. To be fair, they did take a lot of drugs.

The job of the funeral jester was to run alongside the funeral procession dancing and making a fool of himself. He would also run up to members of the mourning party and make jokes at the deceased's expense, all of which just screams respect for the dead. At the funeral of the emperor Vespasian, the official clown was recorded to have made jokes about the exorbitant cost of the funeral and said it would have been better to throw the body in the river and save the country the money.

In 2009, two part-time clowns formed Dead Happy Ireland, the modern equivalent of this Roman jester fest, which has been billed as the "premier funeral clown company." Founder John Brady got the idea when he joked that he would like to be buried in his clown costume, because it obviously wasn't enough for him to terrify people just in this lifetime. Although none of the funeral directors that the clowns surveyed remember ever having a request for clowns at a funeral—probably because no one in Ireland has ever managed to get drunk enough to make that seem like a good idea—Brady and his partner went ahead with their plans. Now if you live on the Emerald Isle you can hire a professional clown for a wake, funeral, or graveside service, all for the low, low price of about $150. Brady assures potential clients that guests will appreciate the attempts at levity, and all the standard clown tricks will be used, "We bring squirting flowers, we make balloon animals. We can even fall into the grave if you want us to. Let your loved one go down with a smile." And send all the guests home screaming, obviously. Unfortunately, this trend seems to be catching on and there are rumors of mourning clowns plying their trade in Eastern Europe, including one whose specialty is to fart loudly during particularly sad parts of the service. Classy.

**IF YOU LIVE TO THE AGE OF 100 YOU HAVE IT MADE, BECAUSE VERY FEW PEOPLE DIE PAST THE AGE OF 100.**

GEORGE BURNS, COMEDIAN (DIED 1996—AT THE AGE OF 100)

# CRASHING YOUR OWN FUNERAL

We've all been there. You go out with some friends to have a few drinks, end up on an all-night bender, and wake up in a ditch to find out you're supposed to be dead. Okay, that might be slight exaggeration of your craziest night out, but as one Brazilian man found out in 2009, getting too drunk to reassure people you are not dead can lead to one awkward funeral.

Fifty-nine-year-old Brazilian bricklayer Ademir Jorge Goncalves didn't tell his family he was spending the night drinking at a truck stop, and they had no idea where he was. This became a problem when a man resembling Goncalves and wearing similar clothes was killed in a car crash that same night, and the majority of family members who were asked to identify the body confirmed it was their very much still alive relative. In some parts of the world this all could have been easily cleared up once Goncalves slept off his hangover, but in accordance with Brazilian tradition the funeral took place the next day.

By then, Goncalves had woken up (probably smelling like death, but most certainly still alive) and when he got back to town was informed that not only was he supposed to be dead but that he was missing his own funeral. He immediately rushed off to stop the service. Adding to the craziness was that it was the Brazilian Day of the Dead, which means he was basically about to show up alive at his own funeral on Halloween. If you can't think of anything that would freak out people more, you are right. The shock of seeing Goncalves walk through the doors of the Funeraria Rainha das Colinas funeral home in the middle of the service scared some of his relatives so badly they tried to jump out of the windows, which, had they succeeded, would have at least meant someone in the family got to use the coffin that day. The owner of the home said he had never seen anything like it in ten years in business. We can only hope Goncalves had the presence of mind to throw open the doors and say something clever in a moment most people will never get the chance to experience.

***Adding to the craziness was that it was the Brazilian Day of the Dead, which means [Goncalves] was basically about to show up alive at his own funeral on Halloween. If you can't think of anything that would freak out people more, you are right.***

Afterward, some of the attendees said they had had doubts about the identity of the deceased. At the funeral Goncalves's mother refused to believe it was her son in the coffin. The funeral director put the misidentification down to the fact that people don't like to look at dead bodies for very long, especially ones that have been so mutilated in car accidents that no one can be sure who they are. It's understandable really.

Other than the whole being dead thing, there was good news for the corpse, as that same day a family reported their son missing. The body was returned to them and presumably finally buried under the correct name.

## DRIVE-THRU FUNERAL HOMES

The ease of attending a funeral without getting out of your car might sound like a great idea in today's fast-paced world, but the idea for a drive-thru funeral home is actually forty-five years old. Thornton's Mortuary in Atlanta introduced society to their new take on mourning in 1968. Five big rooms at the front of the parlor had large glass windows allowing those on the outside to see in. Cars would crawl down the driveway and mourners would pay their respects. If they wanted to leave a message of condolence, boxes were placed outside each window to drop cards into.

Another city soon seized on the idea, but for a very different reason. In 1974, gang violence in Compton, a neighborhood of Los Angeles, started spilling over into funerals. When a gang member was killed, the rival gang knew his funeral would be an easy place to take out more people. The retaliations escalated and put innocent family members in the line of fire. Robert Lee Adams Sr. saw a gap in the market, as well as a way to keep people safer. He opened his own drive-thru funeral home, complete with a floor-to-ceiling bulletproof window for the viewings, and in doing so created a local landmark. People other than gang members were soon requesting drive-thru visitations for their loved ones and, in some cases, for themselves. The parlor has hosted the funerals of various local politicians and important community members, since the number of people who can view the bodies is limited only by the flow of traffic. Even in death there is no escaping gridlock in Los Angeles.

Soon half a dozen other funeral homes with never-leave-your-car options sprouted up around America, including ones in Florida and Louisiana. Then in 1987, a mortician in Chicago added some technology to the drive-thru experience. While other homes were limited by how many rooms they had with windows and their hours of operations, the Gatling Funeral home installed outside screens to view bodies inside twenty-four hours a day. While Mr. Gatling has said he is offended by the comparison to a fast food drive-thru, it is hard not to see the similarities. In order to see the body, the driver pushes a button and "orders" from one of the home's workers. The deceased then pops up on the screen for three seconds, but by pushing the button again and again viewers are allowed to look as long as they want—or at least until the person waiting behind them honks.

While these drive-thru visitations never really caught on nationwide, some people are still heralding them as the future of paying your respects. The benefits are obvious: the elderly don't have to get out of their cars, people who would normally be too uncomfortable to attend funerals might be less frightened, and children can't disrupt the service. You also don't have to worry about finding parking in the middle of a city, and it allows people who work odd hours to mourn at their convenience. And perhaps most importantly, no one is forced to be in a room with relatives who are already feuding over the will.

**DEATH IS NOT THE END. THERE REMAINS THE LITIGATION OVER THE ESTATE.**

AMBROSE BIERCE, WRITER (DIED 1913)

# MODERN-DAY MUMMIES

Natural mummification, where a person is found to be more or less intact many years after they died, is a nice accident. But few cultures since the ancient Egyptians have made mummification a standard practice. And very few people in modern times are known to have asked to be mummified, but when they have they go all out.

The most famous example of modern mummification is Jeremy Bentham, the English founder of utilitarianism. Bentham believed that people had an unnecessarily morbid concept of death and a useless fear of dissection. He thought that people actually seeing dead bodies in their day-to-day lives would cure society of this, and he actually recommended people have corpses in their gardens to improve their quality of life, reasoning that by being confronted by the realities of death every day people would stop being afraid of it. Obviously a bit bonkers, Bentham left strict instructions in his will that he was to be mummified, and his very open-minded friends went through with it after he died in 1832. The mummification was successful on everything but his skull, and his body is still openly displayed, now with a fake head, wearing robes and sitting on a chair, in a corridor of University College London. It says something good about the English that he is still there; if his body were exhibited at an American college, it would almost certainly be involved in every single fraternity hazing ever.

While Bentham's friends did a pretty good job, they were completely guessing when it came to the best way to actually mummify a human. It wasn't until 2011 that a team of British scientists carried out an experiment that was based on years of research into ancient Egyptian techniques. Of course, the only way to know for sure that you have figured out how to mummify someone is to try it out on a human corpse and, luckily for the scientists, Alan Billis volunteered his body for the project after he was diagnosed with terminal lung cancer. Saying that "if people don't volunteer for anything nothing gets found out," Billis called the experiment "bloody interesting." He died at age sixty-one, and after a three-month drying-out period his body was mummified. The process was videotaped and made into a documentary. While the scientists followed as close as possible the steps that would have been done to the pharaoh Tutankhamen's corpse, they did forgo removing Billis's brain through his nose.

***Of course, the only way to know for sure that you have figured out how to mummify someone is to try it out on a human corpse . . .***

If you think modern mummification might be for you, check out the Summum religion. Founded in 1975 by Claude Nowell, it believes in mummification after death. Nowell even built a giant gold pyramid in Salt Lake City, into which his own mummified body was placed after he passed away in 2008. While few of his followers seemed to have followed suit, his services are quite popular when it comes to preserving pets. The ritual preservation was even granted an IRS exemption as a religious act. The Summum do not appear to charge for their services, but they do ask for donations.

# TERRIBLE GETAWAY VEHICLES

You wouldn't think that 20-foot-long behemoths whose most common occupants are dead would be the ideal cars for joyriding, but car thieves will take what they can get, and some seem to have an affinity for hearses. Every now and then there is a news report of a hearse going missing from a funeral home. While some turn up in pieces, most are discovered abandoned not that far away. It seems the idea of tooling around in a gigantic death box is a lot more fun than the reality.

Sometimes a hearse might seem like the ideal transportation unit for something other than bodies; in 1986 an Italian man stole sixteen sheep and then realized he needed a way to take them away, so he stole a hearse as well. Despite how ridiculous the sight of a hearse stuffed with live sheep must have been, the man was only arrested after he was pulled over for speeding.

While it happens less often, sometimes the cars are abandoned for obvious reasons. You see, coffins are heavy, and embalmed bodies can be left in most temperatures for a few hours, which means that every now and then when a car thief decides that a hearse is the perfect score for him or her, they get another person coming along for the ride. In 2010, two men in Cleveland thought a hearse would be great to haul off some computers they had looted from a crematorium, but they found the vehicle occupied. Undeterred, they drove around for a bit before they finally managed to push the body out. Perhaps feeling guilty, they eventually abandoned the hearse, along with a note to the police about where to find the body. It was recovered undamaged.

Another corpse was not so lucky. In 2011, a woman left stranded in front of a funeral home at night after a fight with her girlfriend thought a hearse with the keys still in the ignition was a godsend. When she was apprehended still driving the vehicle three hours later officers discovered that her erratic driving and possible attempts to move the corpse had caused serious damage to the late eighty-five-year-old woman.

But perhaps the ballsiest hearse theft in history was in 1986, when Raymond Allston from Stockton, California, stole a hearse and body during the funeral procession itself. After running alongside the car for a few minutes, Allston jumped in and lay down on top of the casket. Obviously confused, the driver and passenger bailed out of the hearse. Allston then climbed in the front seat and drove away. He managed to drive several miles, even losing the police at one point, before he crashed into a parked car. Others in the funeral procession were apparently unaware that anything had happened, and the funeral went on as planned, only fifteen minutes behind schedule.

**DEATH IS THE LAST ENEMY: ONCE WE'VE GOT PAST THAT I THINK EVERYTHING WILL BE ALRIGHT.**

ALICE THOMAS ELLIS, AUTHOR (DIED 2005)

## CRAZY CREMATIONS

Considering the job description involves simply taking dead bodies and burning them, the cremation business has a surprising number of scandals to its name. Even after society came around to viewing cremation as perfectly acceptable, some in the industry managed to screw it up for everyone.

One of the more obvious problems with the practice is that not everything burns. And some of the inflammable things in the human body are worth money. With gold prices going through the roof, six workers at five different South Korean crematories decided to supplement their incomes by stealing and then selling the gold teeth they found mixed in with the ashes. One worker managed to net himself almost $20,000 before being caught. And if you think it should have been obvious to the gold dealers where these people were getting so many teeth, you are right. The police arrested three additional men for purchasing the ill-gotten gold.

> ***One of the more obvious problems with [cremation] is that not everything burns. And some of the inflammable things in the human body are worth money.***

But the most disturbing crime committed by some crematoriums is giving customers back the remains of someone, or something, other than their loved ones. One of the more obvious signs you have not been given your grandma's ashes is when you receive them before the date on the cremation certificate. The All State Cremation service in Florida was shut down in 2004 after one woman noticed that part of the legally binding form had been altered with Wite-Out. When she looked into it, she found out her family had received the ashes six days before their relative had been cremated.

At least she received human remains. In the most famous crematorium scandal ever, customers were given who knows what in urns. It certainly wasn't human. In 2002, the Environmental Protection Agency responded to complaints that something weird was going on at the Tri-State Crematory in Georgia. Within minutes of arriving, the scale of what they were witnessing became apparent. Rather than putting the bodies in the oven as he was being paid to do, the owner was dumping them around his property. It appeared to have been going on for years, since the bodies they found were in all stages of decomposition, some basically skeletons. Of the 2,000 bodies sent to the crematorium, 339 of them appeared to have been dumped. The owner, Ray Brent Marsh, claimed that the oven was broken, but when tested it proved to be in working order. Only 224 of the discarded corpses were even identified and the families informed. Marsh was eventually charged with 787 criminal counts, as well as facing a class action lawsuit brought by the families.

The only thing that can be said for Marsh is that he kept the bodies outside. In 2002, a Spanish crematory worker was arrested after he was pulled over with the partial remains of nineteen corpses in his car. A search of his home revealed another thirteen, which had apparently been in his possession for at least four years. He may have gotten them from his former boss, who was already under investigation after fifty corpses had been found in his house.

# REAL-LIFE *WEEKEND AT BERNIE'S*

You might assume that the events that went down in the 1989 cult classic *Weekend at Bernie's* could never come true, but you would be wrong. Apparently there really are people who, upon finding someone apparently dead, will not call an ambulance but will party with the corpse.

In 2011, Robert Young walked into his friend Jeffrey Jarrett's house and found him unresponsive. While Young swears he had no idea Jarrett was dead, carrying his limp friend out to the car and driving to a bar with him doesn't make much sense in almost any possible situation. On the way Young stopped to pick up another friend, Mark Rubinson, who, fortunately, he found completely alert. The two bundled into the car with their dead friend and hit the town. First they stopped by a bar to drink to Jarrett's memory. All that sorrow must have made them hungry because then they went for nachos. And finally, they went to a strip club, because the only real way to honor someone's passing is lap dances. Unfortunately for the late Mr. Jarrett, he had to stay in the car for all of the fun. This was made doubly unfair by the fact that his still-alive-and-kicking friends had borrowed his credit card for the night and all the strippers and drinks were on him.

At 4 A.M., a mere five hours after Young had found the body, they took it back home and tucked it in bed, before flagging down a police officer to tell him something might be wrong with their friend. Despite the men's protestations that they had no idea it was anything as serious as death, the police report stated that Jarrett was "obviously deceased." Once they figured out exactly what had happened, the police arrested the two men for identity theft, criminal impersonation, and abuse of a corpse. The men would eventually plead guilty to the lesser charges. Jarrett was not available for comment.

***[S]ome determined relatives have been known to force the remains of their loved one into large suitcases, giving a whole new meaning to family baggage.***

And while Jarrett's friends never tried to convince anyone that Jarrett was alive, people do that, too, and a lot more often than you would think. The problem is that it is not cheap to ship a body long distances. When faced with the sudden demise of a relative hundreds or thousands of miles away from where they are going to be buried, many people will try to get them onto planes by claiming they are alive. Flight attendants know the warning signs: an older person, usually slightly gray, who is wearing sunglasses and "sleeping," being pushed by a younger person. However, a man in Miami got a little more creative by trying to sneak his mother on in a garment bag, and some determined relatives have been known to force the remains of their loved ones into large suitcases, giving a whole new meaning to family baggage.

# WHERE THERE'S A WILL . . .

Once you are dead you don't get much say in, well, anything. Unless your friends and family are really into Ouija boards, you lose the right to complain about stuff as soon as you keel over. Legally your family doesn't even have to carry out whatever funeral plans you asked for; if you always wanted to be shot into space but they think that is a waste of money, too bad for you. So in order to have control after you die you have two options: (1) figure out how to come back as a ghost and haunt your relatives until they do what you want, or (2) leave a completely insane will.

The "Queen of Mean," Leona Helmsley, famously left her entire fortune to her dog, an act that is more common than you would think. And a Canadian lawyer named Charles Vance Millar set off a mini baby boom in Toronto when he left most of his estate to whichever local woman gave birth to the most children in the ten years after his death. Four women managed to have nine children each in that time and split the prize. But when it comes to screwing over your relatives, no one even comes close to Wellington R. Burt.

The lumber baron was worth almost $100 million when he died in 1919, or $1.2 billion in today's money. As relatives of one of the ten richest men in America, his family no doubt looked forward to the reading of the will. They were about to get the shock of their lives. Of his seven children, he had only ever really liked one, and apparently Burt didn't really even care for him all that much. To screw over his abhorred family, Burt included a "spite clause" in his will. He left his children a couple thousand dollars each (less than what his housekeeper got), but he didn't want to give the rest of his fortune away to charity. No, he wanted the money to stay in the family, just not with any members of the family he had actually known. So his will stipulated that his fortune be held in trust, where his children and grandchildren couldn't touch it, until twenty-one years after the last grandchild who was alive at the time of his death had died. That condition was finally met in 2011 and, after a bit of legal wrangling, twelve of his descendents, aged nineteen to ninety-four, split his considerable fortune between them. Talk about cashing in!

**THE IDEA IS TO DIE YOUNG AS LATE AS POSSIBLE.**

ASHLEY MONTAGU, ANTHROPOLOGIST (DIED 1999)

# THE VAGINA CARVER

The sad reality of death is that no matter how much you love someone, over time your memory of him or her starts fading. Fortunately, while we live we have the technology to be able to record voices and take pictures, meaning you can hold on to a detailed image of a person for years after they die. But for one woman in Serbia that wasn't enough. She wanted to make sure her husband had a very literal, *very* concrete reminder of her anatomy.

Before Milena Marinkovic died she decided that she never wanted her husband of fifty years to forget one aspect of their marriage—their sex life. Milena left her beloved husband a letter detailing her last request, which was for him to have her vagina engraved on her tombstone. Just in case he couldn't explain the correct likeness to a stoneworker, she supplied some very personal photos as well as detailed instructions. Her stated goal was for her husband to refrain from chasing after women once she died—although honestly the pictures would probably have been a more logical keepsake in that case, rather than a stone carving a couple miles away from his home.

Milena's husband, Milan, decided to honor the request, but it was more difficult than he expected. When he told engravers he wanted his wife's private parts depicted in a small area on the back of her large tombstone, most of them found the idea blasphemous and turned him down. Finally the determined seventy-two-year-old found a man who agreed to carve the body part into the tombstone. Milan was happy with the work, saying it was a very good likeness. We can only hope his evaluation ended there.

While the engraving is pretty obvious once you know what it is, there is no escaping the fact that it looks more like a trilobite (one of those fossils that look like giant woodlice) than a vagina. The ambiguity of the carving has come in handy though, like when the deceased's brother saw the engraving for the first time and mistook it for a bird with a large beak. His brother-in-law chose not to correct him rather than point out it was a representation of his sister's vagina, there for everyone in the cemetery to see for hundreds of years. And come they have, with Milan saying people from other funerals now wander over to his wife's grave all the time to see her labia. It's certainly one way to spice up an otherwise dour event.

## THE WEIRD WORLD OF OBITUARIES

When someone you love—or at least someone who happens to be related to you through cosmic happenstance—dies, you may suddenly find yourself forced to sum up his or her life in a couple hundred words for the public to read. While death announcements have been standard for many hundreds of years, it was only in the 1800s that Britain and the United States started expanding them to include interesting personal information about the deceased. And like anything the Victorians did with death, they went overboard: The longest obituary ever was that of Queen Victoria herself, which ran to over 16,000 words.

We can assume the Queen's obituary was pretty straightforward and included nothing but nice things about her. This is of course the standard, since most people frown on remembering the dead by straight-up insulting them. But journalists have long had a code to imply unsavory things about a person while seeming to be perfectly pleasant. For example, "died suddenly" often implies suicide, while "a boisterous personality" usually means a drunk. However, some obituaries don't even bother with any sort of subtle code. When Dolores Aguilar died in 2008, none of her forty-eight descendents managed to come up with a single nice thing to say about her, and instead a California newspaper ran the following obit:

"*Dolores had no hobbies, made no contribution to society, and rarely shared a kind word or deed in her life. I speak for the majority of her family when I say her presence will not be missed by many, very few tears will be shed and there will be no lamenting over her passing . . . There will be no service, no prayers and no closure for the family she spent a lifetime tearing apart.*"

Ouch!

Oddly enough, numerous people have lived to read their own obituaries. Pope John Paul II saw three of them incorrectly published before papers finally got it right in 2005. CNN.com once mistakenly ran Fidel Castro's obit, which besides being wrong about the whole dead dictator thing also said he was a "lifeguard, athlete, and movie star." The Jamaican political leader Marcus Garvey was actually killed by his own obituary. After he suffered a series of strokes his death was falsely reported in the paper. Garvey was so upset by the negative tone of the piece (among other things, it said he had died "broke, alone, and unpopular") that the stress actually killed him. Maybe worse than speaking ill of the dead is speaking dead of the ill.

# FROZEN DEAD GUY DAYS

Bredo Morstoel died in 1989. An early proponent of the cryonics movement, he requested his body be stored in deep freeze in a California facility. But because his relatives were even weirder than he was, Morstoel didn't stay there for long. In 1993, his grandson Trygve Bauge took the body and moved it to Nederland, Colorado. The one problem with this plan was that the small mountain town didn't actually have a cryonics institute at which to keep the frozen corpse. But Bauge wasn't concerned. Apparently thinking that he could do just as good a job as the professionals, he set his grandfather's body up in a shack behind his mother's house.

Somehow he and his mom managed to keep this a secret, even though every month they paid a guy to haul 1,700 pounds of dry ice to the shack to keep granddad frozen. It was only after Bauge, a Norwegian citizen, was thrown out of the country for overstaying his visa and his mother was threatened with eviction that the truth came out. Despite the fact that she was being thrown out of her home because she had failed to install electricity or plumbing, her real concern was that leaving meant Morstoel's body would almost certainly warm up before they found a new home for it.

A newspaper reported the story, and instead of being totally freaked out by a corpse on ice, the locals rallied to keep him there. While the local council passed a new law (which they now realized was necessary for some reason) that basically said, "Hey, no keeping dead people in your homes," they also literally included a grandfather clause saying that Morstoel's body could stay.

The town embraced their frozen dead guy, with local businesses donating money and equipment for his makeshift cryogenics shed, and Nederland started a yearly celebration in his honor, aptly called Frozen Dead Guy Days. Over a long weekend in March, locals and tourists have dead guy lookalike contests, coffin races, even tours of Morstoel's shed. Despite being hugely popular and drawing 10,000 visitors every year, the celebrations are in trouble. In 2012, Bo Shaffer, who had the job of hauling almost a ton of dry ice to the shed every month for eighteen years, insisted on a raise to cover rising fuel costs for his four-hour trip as well as the increasing price of dry ice. When his request was refused he threatened to quit. Shaffer says he feels bad, but he insists this is the only way he will get the attention his job deserves. When he heard about the situation, Bauge, now back in the United States, retaliated by threatening to move his grandfather's body to a proper facility in Michigan. Meanwhile the townsfolk insist that though they will miss their frozen dead guy the celebrations will continue without him. After all, the show must go on.

## WOULD YOU LIKE A COFFIN WITH THAT?

If there is one kind of business that will never be hurting for customers, it is funeral parlors. No matter how many amazing medical advances are made, everyone is going to die eventually, and the growing population just means that even more people will need mortuary services in the future. But this guaranteed clientele hasn't stopped some funeral homes from looking for new and slightly bizarre ways to expand their services.

Some funeral directors started out small: one parlor in Pennsylvania installed a children's room. Why so many people were bringing their children to help pick out coffins is a different discussion, but in order to make it easier on the little ones the room is full of toys and happy colors, and Disney movies are played on a TV. Which Disney movies play is key, though; if anyone ever shows *Bambi* in there those children will be messed up for life.

But it's not just kids who get stressed out in funeral homes. Adults would probably love a place to relax as well—or at least that is what one funeral director in South Carolina put his money on. While Chris Robinson's business had always offered a warm cup of coffee to grieving relatives while they sorted out funeral plans, after a renovation he realized he had some extra room in his building: exactly enough room for a Starbucks. While he didn't go so far as to add a neon mermaid sign under his funeral home's name, his baristas are all Starbucks trained and wear the iconic green aprons. And don't worry, in case you happen to be passing and crave a cup of joe but haven't lost a loved one recently, there is also a separate entrance for the general public to come in and place an order.

If people come for coffee, a Massachusetts funeral home hopes they will be tempted by chili. Terry Probst wants his funeral home to become an active part of community life so that when people have to show up to, you know, actually mourn someone, they will already be used to the building and feel comfortable there. To this end he hosts chili cook-offs and murder mystery nights on site. He is not alone in trying to make better use of his space when no one has died; funeral homes around the country are trying to rebrand themselves as the perfect spaces for all types of parties—not just really depressing ones.

This outreach is not just limited to America either. As Greece's economy collapsed, many soccer teams in the country lost their corporate sponsors. One funeral parlor stepped up to lend financial support to its local team, only asking the squad to wear black uniforms with a cross and the macabre logo of the undertaker on them. Players say the creepy look has actually worked for them, the opposing teams being too freaked out to pay full attention to the matches. Sounds like a win-win.

# NOTHING IS CERTAIN BUT SPORTS AND FUNERALS

Sports fans are insane. The most dedicated ones cover their bodies in tattoos of their favorite teams, sell their plasma to afford season tickets, and even name their children after the heroes of whatever game they follow. But every now and then you find someone for whom a lifetime dedication is not enough, and his support continues on to the grave.

When Ohio State fan Roy Miracle died his family wanted one last show of school spirit from him. Laid out in his open casket, he made the perfect "I" in OHIO, and three of his family members provided the other letters, all while smiling widely. The image went viral, but many fans questioned why Roy was buried in such a boring casket if he was such a huge fan.

You see, there is a surprisingly lucrative business in making sports-themed caskets and urns. Most big college teams are available, with some of the more rabid fan bases, like Texas A&M, having entire websites dedicated just to funeral paraphernalia for alumni who have gone to that big football field in the sky. While some of the coffins allow for a more subtle showing of support by having the team name embroidered into the inside of the casket, others, particularly NASCAR-themed coffins for some reason, are completely adorned inside and out with logos—and a checkered flag indicating you have come to the end of your race.

But no matter how obsessed your average football or baseball fan may be, they have nothing on people who follow soccer. In some countries people are sent to their graves because of what team they support, and perhaps nowhere is the beautiful game deadlier than Colombia. National player Andrés Escobar was even murdered, seemingly for scoring a goal on his own team during the 1994 World Cup match. But one teenager, also from Columbia, reversed this trend. After being killed in 2011 during his own local soccer match, seventeen-year-old Christopher Jacome's friends decided he needed to attend at least one more match of his favorite team. Somehow they managed to get Jacome's coffin past security and into the stadium, where they held it aloft for the entire ninety minutes. While it was a nice show of devotion to their young friend, the soccer club was unimpressed and launched an investigation into how the corpse was let into the stadium. As the club medic said, "This is the only part of the world where this has happened." Clearly the medic hadn't been to a Meatloaf concert.

## ONE FOOT IN THE CAGE

While the idea that most people should be given a proper and respectful funeral when they die spans all times and cultures, there is also a long-standing desire to see that bad people get the exact opposite. And we mean "see" literally (most people secretly like a good train wreck). Throughout history, when undesirables and criminals got their final comeuppance, people from otherwise civilized societies turned out in droves to have a good look at those unburied dead bodies.

Even in places where public executions were rare, public displays of executed corpses were not. In Roman times crucified bodies were left lining the roads into cities. Ancient tribes in France and England hung the bodies of executed captives from trees. But by the Renaissance European countries were building special areas and structures just to make sure that people got their fill of dead criminals on a daily basis and the point was pretty clear—don't do anything illegal yourself or you won't get to be buried in hallowed ground.

Gibbets, sort of gallows for already dead people to hang off of, were constructed on the hills above towns so that displayed bodies could be seen from anywhere, and many cities lined their bridges or walls with heads impaled on spikes. And, if someone did a very bad thing, his entire body might be displayed in a cage above a city gate or waterway. A person didn't even need to be executed to be displayed this way; Oliver Cromwell was responsible for the execution of Charles I and then went on to die a natural death, but when the monarchy in England was returned to power they were still pretty pissed at him and had his body dug up and displayed anyway.

This trend wasn't limited to Europe. Australia, Canada, and some Middle Eastern countries also displayed their less popular dead. Usually this was as a warning to others not to be equally as naughty. Pirates were especially likely to be subjected to post-death display, with their heads and bodies strung up at the entrances to ports as a warning to anyone else who might be thinking of shanghaiing a ship. In case there weren't enough criminals to keep the cages full, some bodies were submerged in tar before being displayed so they would last years longer.

> ***Pirates were especially likely to be subjected to post-death display, with their heads and bodies strung up at the entrances to ports as a warning to anyone else who might be thinking of shanghaiing a ship.***

Of course not everyone was a fan of these displays. Imagine having to see an increasingly rotted body every day on your way to work? Well, people felt the same way about that 500 years ago as they would now. During the 1800s most countries finally decided that this tradition was not only pretty sadistic but also smelly and unhygienic.

Even though most countries don't officially sanction gibbets anymore, that doesn't mean that bad guys don't still get displayed after they die. Mussolini's body was hung upside down for Italians to kick and spit on in Milan after his execution in 1945. More recently, technology has taken the place of cages, and images of the executed bodies of Saddam Hussein and Muammar Gaddafi went viral online. When Osama bin Laden was killed a significant number of people were upset when no image of his dead body was released. But never fear, when technology fails to entertain us with the unfortunate corpses of the criminally minded, there's always *Here Comes Honey Boo Boo.*

## A



## B

## C

## D



## E

# F



# G

## H



## I



## J



## K

# L



# M

# T

**Kathy Benjamin**'s writing has received more than 100 million hits across some of the most popular humor and trivia websites in the world. Her work has been featured on sites like Cracked, Mental Floss, Pajiba, Uproxx, Playboy's The Smoking Jacket, and in *Reader's Digest* and *Mental Floss* magazine. You can find her debut science fiction novel, *Level 15*, at JukePop Serials. She lives in Texas with her husband and evil bunny rabbit.

12642698R00142

Printed in Great Britain
by Amazon.co.uk, Ltd.,
Marston Gate.